ENDING WAR

Transcending A Primitive Practice That Has No Place in The Modern World

Copyright © 2022 Alice Karwitha

All rights reserved. No part of this publication may be reproduced, distributed, or transmitted in any form or by any means, including photocopying, recording, or other electronic or mechanical methods, without the prior written permission of the publisher, except in the case of brief quotations embodied in critical reviews and certain other non-commercial uses permitted by copyright law.

ISBN: 9798355662875

DEDICATION

To Naomi Mumbi, Andrew Mureithi
and Terry Kathambi

Table of Contents

Chapter 1

A Planet at War with Itself

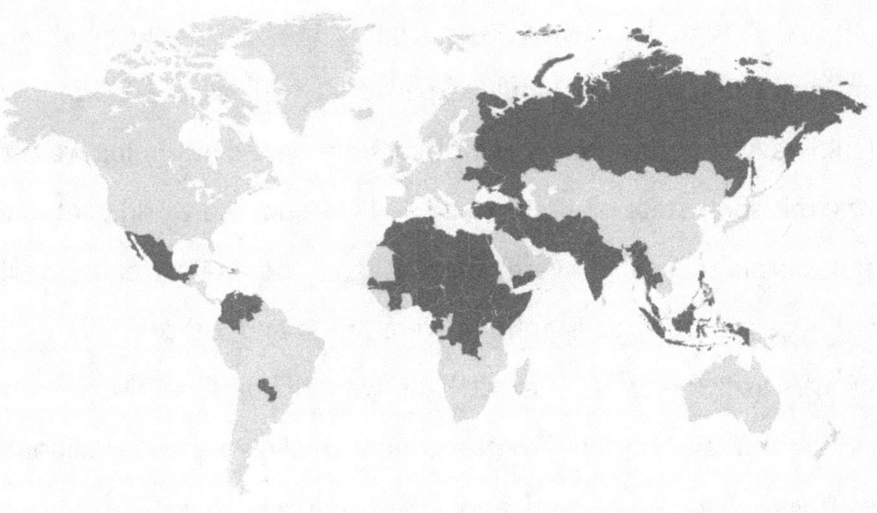

Source: https://www.statista.com/chart/21652/countries-with-armed-clashes-reported/

Many parts of the world are currently engaged in war, although you wouldn't know this from listening to the mainstream media. The mainstream media does not highlight this alarming state of affairs. While we are treated to almost non-stop news on everything from celebrities to sports, we never get to see the same journalistic zeal when it comes to the much more important topic of the wars being fought on the planet. Further, the reporting of war by the mainstream media makes it seem as if war is a normal part of life. Any analysis of the situation is done from the assumption that war is normal; there is never any questioning of the status quo. They analyse everything from the weapons employed to which side is winning, but they never question why war is a normal part of life on this planet. And so, we learn to live with this reality. We push it to the back of our minds and continue with life. You would expect that with all these wars, we would have serious debates and discussions aimed at finding ways to bring this sorry state of affairs to an end. But no, the world continues as if nothing unusual were happening. The mainstream media continues reporting as if nothing were amiss and we continue living our lives as if the world is exactly the way it should be. There is no alarm or dismay, only indifference as innocent lives are lost, livelihoods destroyed, people maimed and cities reduced to rubble while a disinterested world moves on. A new day dawns and we rush to our jobs and live our lives without a thought spared for the people being killed in distant parts of the world, sometimes by our governments and our militaries and paid for by our taxes.

Can you imagine living life knowing that at any time a bomb could hit your house and kill you and everyone inside? This is how people in some parts of the world live. Where is our outrage as citizens of the planet? Why aren't we out there protesting what our governments are doing? We are programmed to accept this as normal. Surely the time has come to break free of this programming, to wake up to the horror in which our brothers and sisters in other parts of the world have to exist.   We are all conditioned to accept war as normal including the ones who join the military in the mistaken belief that this is a noble duty, something they need to do to defend their countries from the "enemy". But who made the people on the other side of the world our enemy? Who made that decision on our behalf? How did we come to accept that some bureaucrat in an office could decide that someone on the other side of the planet is our enemy for whatever reason their deranged mind could come up with?

The End Justifies the Means

One of the main justifications for war is the idea that the end justifies the means. In other words, some goals are so important and so noble that it is justified to use any means necessary to achieve them. So, for example, to stop Russia from invading Ukraine, it is justified to go to war, perhaps even nuclear war. To stop China from invading Taiwan, it is justified to go to war. To bring democracy to the people, it is justified to forcefully change regimes even if it results in civil war. Am I the only one who thinks this logic is problematic? Surely, there has to be a limit to what one can or should do to achieve a goal. If the price is too high and completely outweighs the benefit, it is time to abandon that goal. No end can be so critical that it justifies mass murder. This mindset is a rabbit hole that leads one so far away from reason that by the time they wake up to how far they have gone, they will be firmly in the terrain of insanity. One of the biggest problems we have on this planet is that there are extremely powerful people in positions of authority who are completely trapped in this way of thinking. They are so blinded by ambition and greed that they long ago lost their humanity, empathy and compassion. The suffering of people does not move them. They are completely lost in the mindset that the ends justify the means and they are dragging all of us to our collective doom. Our only hope is to reject this way of thinking and stand united against those who claim to be our leaders yet only have their selfish interests at heart. If we continue blindly down this path, the end will be the destruction of our planet. Since these blind leaders have no hope or possibility of waking themselves up, *we* have to be the ones to wake up and save ourselves.

I remember as a child thinking about war and marvelling at how human beings could inflict so much pain and suffering on each other. Reading through accounts of war such as the two world wars, I couldn't understand how human beings could do such things to each other. I remember hearing about the Iran-Iraq war and wondering to myself how two countries whose names sounded so similar they could very well be siblings, could be at war with each other. My young mind just couldn't comprehend it. I remember pondering the evils of war and thinking to myself that no wonder only men went to war, because no mother would want her children to suffer so much. Even at such a tender age, I could see the senselessness of war. I remember thinking that people only went to war because they were manipulated as it was clear that no one would ever go to war willingly.

So why do we allow our governments to make decisions on our behalf that cause us so much suffering? I believe it is because we have been manipulated into a mindset that sees other people as enemies. Our leaders keep pointing at others and making us believe they are a threat to us. To protect ourselves from them, we are told that we need to fight them either politically or physically. Our leaders manipulate us into fearing the "other" who is labelled as a threat and once we start fearing, we stop using logic. When we stop using logic, we become susceptible to all manner of ideas including the mindset that the end justifies the means. We allow our leaders to lead us down a path whose end is death. If we could instead reject fear and refuse to accept the idea that other people are a threat to us and see them as our brothers and sisters, we would never allow ourselves to be manipulated into going to war against them. We would imagine how it would feel if someone dropped bombs on our country and we would instantly see that no argument could justify this.

Can good come out of evil?

Before we can even begin to answer this question, we must first agree on one thing. Is war evil? Take a moment to think about this. Do you believe that war is evil? Do you believe that war is sometimes justified? When is it justified? Many of us have been so deceived by the belief that war is sometimes acceptable or even inevitable that we do not take the time to carefully consider this question. We have been programmed to accept that war is something that will always be with us, something we all hate but which is an inevitable part of the world we live in. But do you understand that this indifferent attitude towards war is a learned attitude? An attitude we've been programmed to default to? Because of the casual way war is treated by the media and some of our leaders, we learn to accept that it is something that will always be with us. We will later see how this programming is achieved, but the first thing we need to realize is that this is programming and as with any programming, it can be overcome.

Most people would agree that killing other human beings is evil, which is why we have laws against it. No society would ever allow its inhabitants to kill each other and this is a basic principle that most societies live by. So, if the killing of one person results in serious punishment, why is it that mass murder is considered acceptable? How did we as a planet get to the point where we accept as normal that a group of people called the military, whose sole purpose and training is killing should exist? Aren't we supposed to be evolving into higher levels of consciousness? We should be eliminating the primitive practice of killing each other, but instead, we attempt to make it more advanced, more civilized and more sanitized. This is an impossibility and no amount of artificial intelligence or drones that attempt to sanitize war will ever make it acceptable. Just because we are not fighting with crude weapons like swords and spears doesn't make war any less primitive.

It should be obvious to everyone that war is evil, but just the fact that we have to spend some time delving into the question of whether or not war is evil goes to show just how much we have become victims of programming. The fact that it is not immediately obvious to everyone that war is evil is a reminder of how much our thinking, our assumptions and our beliefs have been programmed. If you genuinely feel that war is justified in some situations, then you might need to consider that you are the victim of programming i.e., the "ends justify the means" programming. And why has this mindset affected us so much that we can no longer assume that we are all operating from the same basic standpoint that all life is precious and should not be taken away under any circumstances? It is because there are people in our midst who benefit greatly from this mindset and they push it aggressively and relentlessly upon the rest of us. We have to reject this mindset and break free of it and go back to the inner knowing that life is a precious gift that should be respected by all. Breaking free of this programming is the beginning of our collective healing as a planet and this is what will allow us to eliminate the evil that is war from our midst.

War Supports Women's Rights

When the United States withdrew its forces from Afghanistan, there was an immediate outcry against the withdrawal and one of the reasons given was that the women of Afghanistan were being abandoned and their rights would be taken away by the Taliban. This false logic is simply mind-boggling and the fact that the mainstream media so shamelessly pressed this point is a reminder of just how far we have strayed from sanity. The United States army was responsible for the murder of many civilians during its twenty years in Afghanistan and the idea that it supported women's rights must surely be a cruel joke to the people whose lives were destroyed. I wonder what the women of Afghanistan whose rights were supposedly being defended would have to say about the insane idea that the twenty-year war was somehow good for them. This kind of sick logic has been employed time and time again on this planet to justify all sorts of evil. It is almost as if the people advancing these ideas have never heard of peaceful ways of achieving things. I wonder how the journalists who were eagerly reporting about Afghan women's rights would feel if *their* countries were bombed in the name of fighting for women's rights. Why the hypocrisy? How could anyone possibly justify such an argument? If war is something you would not want for yourself, why would you want it for someone else or imagine that someone else would want it for themselves?

Can war ever be used to support women's rights? Of course not! What if, instead of spending trillions on the war in Afghanistan, the United

States instead utilized this money to invest in the country in various ways and empowered the people by strengthening the education of both girls and boys? Let's imagine that this was done over twenty years. Where would Afghanistan be today? Would it be the devastated country it is today? How long would it be before the people's mindset changed and they no longer wanted the Taliban? Eventually, through education and the raising of the standards of living, the people themselves would have liberated themselves from the Taliban. There would be no need for war. But as long as powerful countries like the United States continue thinking by default that war and regime change are the only options and are not willing to consider any other peaceful options, they will keep dragging the whole planet downwards while telling themselves that they are the most advanced nations on earth.

War brings peace

This sounds positively Orwellian, but it is a justification that is used by some countries to go to war. Consider the war that has been taking place in the Sahel (Mali, Niger, Chad, Mauritania and Burkina Faso). To help bring peace to the region, France sent their military to help the locals fight the terrorists. So, what happens when you send the military of a more advanced nation to support locals? The answer is obviously that you prolong the war, you bring in more sophisticated weapons and you attract the interest of other actors who may want to support the opposite side for whatever geopolitical objectives they may have. In the end, the only thing that is accomplished is to make a bad situation even worse. How is it that people who should know better, who are supposedly world leaders could fall for this kind of false logic? Why couldn't France instead try to bring the warring parties together for dialogue? Why not go through the well-respected regional bodies like the ECOWAS or the African Union that could use their influence to bring the parties to the table for dialogue? Why is it that such options are never explored and instead the powerful nations always default to military intervention in the name of bringing peace?

Would an attempt to reach peace through diplomacy work? We don't know, but it would surely be a thousand times better to try something that could fail without making the situation worse than to try something that would invariably make the situation worse. Trying to bring the parties together for dialogue may or may not have the desired result immediately, but at least it would not make the situation worse. Sending armies to supposedly bring peace is guaranteed to make a bad situation worse. The world's most powerful nations need to put aside their egos and their desire to show off their might and simply come in with a desire to help. Their egos only make bad situations worse and this is true in almost every situation where they intervene militarily. There is not one instance in which their interventions shorten the crises but invariably, they make the crises more complicated, more difficult to resolve and last longer than they otherwise would.

I must commend the African Union for its attempts to intervene in the crises that face the African continent by sending representatives to try to negotiate peaceful resolutions. Are they always successful? Not necessarily, as in the case of the Ethiopian civil war, but sometimes they can be a resounding success as in the case of Kenya when the African Union sent Kofi Annan to help negotiate peace after the 2007 post-election violence.   I think there is a lesson here that the world could learn on how to handle conflicts. The idea that a military intervention could bring peace is completely flawed and should be rejected by all. What is needed is to strengthen regional and global institutions that could try to bring the various parties to the table for dialogue or failing this, bring the perpetrators to justice. Bodies such as the International Criminal Court should be embraced by all and not just used by the developed world to dominate the less developed countries. The United Nations should also step up its efforts to bring peace to the planet and it could start by removing the ridiculous notion of a veto for the powerful nations. This veto power has been used to scuttle peaceful resolutions so many times that it's a wonder it is allowed to continue existing. These institutions and others have the potential to change the world by enabling us to find peaceful solutions to conflicts. If we learn how to negotiate with each other, then a time will come when there will be no need to ever take up arms and war will be but a distant memory. This is the only way we will evolve to a higher state of consciousness.

War brings democracy

The idea that war brings democracy has been used as a justification for fighting many wars around the world. The United States as the self-appointed democracy police has used its position as the foremost military power on the planet to force democracy down the throats of people around the world. No doubt democracy is good, but the idea that it is worthwhile to fight a war to bring democracy and freedom to people who don't have it is quite simply unrealistic, to put it mildly. It doesn't take much imagination to realize that there are more efficient ways of bringing democracy to other parts of the world. The first thing is to make sure that democracy is working at home before you purport to export it to other parts of the world. Make sure that all people are free in your country and equal under the law before you attempt to spread democracy to other parts of the world.

What is democracy all about at its core? It is about people putting their differences aside and coming together to agree on how they want to exist. It is about saying that it doesn't matter how different we are, we can find a way to make it work and we can put aside our differences long enough to agree on some basic principles such as how we want to be governed, which freedoms we want to have, which things we don't want in society, etc. It's about finding common ground that brings us together despite our differences. It's about seeing the basic humanity in each of us and agreeing that despite our differences, we want every one of us to live in dignity. Given this basic understanding of democracy, how could someone possibly imagine that it is something you can force on another society? How could war possibly bring about the harmonious co-existence of people? It beats all logic. Democracy comes when people's awareness is raised and this can only happen through education and through observing democracy at work in other places. This is what gives others the vision to want democracy in their own societies.

The idea that democracy is under threat from other ideologies such as communism and therefore there is a need to go to war to protect it is at its core, deceptive. The idea that there is an ideology that is so important that it is necessary to go to war to defend has been the cause of much bloodshed on this planet. How many people died in the Vietnam war that was meant to prevent the spread of communism? How many people died in the holocaust because of the ideology of a superior race? How many countries have gone through colonialism because someone felt that their way of life was superior and therefore had to be forced on everyone? Isn't human life worth more than any ideology? Unfortunately, human beings have been gullible to this lie for a very long time. This is the same lie that caused the cold war, which led us to the brink of nuclear war and we are seeing a revival of this cold war mentality today. The United States is once again attempting to divide the world into two opposing camps. We are seeing an escalation in hostilities between the United States and both Russia and China that is bringing us closer to nuclear war. We should not allow this. If democracy is so good then it should be able to speak for itself. Everyone should be able to see its benefits and want it for themselves. It is not something that should be forced upon the world even to the extent of bringing us to the brink of nuclear war.

Is democracy the only option available on the planet? One cannot argue with the fact that democracy, when it is working properly can be a wonderful system of governance as seen in the Scandinavian countries. It is a system that others would want to emulate when it is working well. But we also have examples of democracy not working well and the United States is a good example. One only needs to look at the polarization of the American people into two antagonistic camps, the Democrats and the Republicans to see that democracy is not working well in this country. We have seen how easily democracy can be subverted by the determined effort to make voting less accessible through the court system in America. We have seen how the rights of people can be systematically suppressed in the United States even while it boasts of being the foremost democracy on the planet. Therefore, democracy is good when it works but it is not the only system of governance and it can certainly be subverted.

Meanwhile, China, a country of more than a billion people has gradually raised hundreds of millions of them out of poverty. They did this not through democracy but through what they call "communism with Chinese characteristics". And what would be so wrong with removing the worst characteristics of communism and creating a system that can raise everyone's standard of living? Is this the direction that poorer parts of the globe should be taking? Why can't we in Africa look at what the Chinese are doing in terms of poverty reduction and ask ourselves whether this is something we can emulate? We could very well take out whatever we don't like about communism, for example, the suppression of individual freedoms and introduce a "communism with African characteristics" which could lift Africa out of poverty.

My point here is that every country, every region and every continent should be free to improve the lives of their populations, no matter which direction this takes them. There should be no big brother playing the role of democracy police, forcing everyone to adopt a system that *they* feel is the best option for everyone. No one should feel that this or that ideology is the only ideology that should exist on the planet and that it must be enforced even if it means war. I wonder what would happen if Africa decided to go the way of China. Would the "defenders of democracy" decide that we ought to be bombed back to the stone age to fight the dangerous spread of communism?

War brings freedom

I wonder how people in countries like Syria, Libya and Iraq feel when they are told that the bombings and mass murders that were unleashed on them were meant to bring them freedom from tyranny. How could war possibly bring freedom? How could anyone who thinks it is okay to kill thousands or millions of people possibly bring freedom to the people? The kind of person who thinks violence is a solution to any problem is someone whose thinking is primitive and backward, no matter what kind of suit they are wearing. Look at a country like Libya. The country had a functioning infrastructure, schools, water and other basic amenities. Life under Gaddafi was comfortable for most Libyans. What happened after the war that supposedly delivered the country from tyranny? Today, the country is a hotbed for terrorism, instability, trafficking, smuggling and civil war. The interference by outside forces did not deliver freedom to the Libyan people; instead, it destroyed a country that was previously stable. Most countries that experienced the so-called "Arab spring" ended up much worse than they were before. What about Syria which was bombed supposedly to liberate it from Bashar al-Assad? Syria is still at war today with interference and weapons flowing in from different actors. Are the Syrian people better off today or should they have been left alone to determine their fate without interference? The results speak for themselves. What about Iraq, how is it faring after the ouster of Saddam Hussein? It remains unstable to this day and is a hotbed for terrorism. These countries ended up much worse than they were before the interventions. The idea that you can intervene militarily in a country to bring freedom and deliverance from tyranny is a false notion that not only doesn't work but leaves a country worse off than it was before. What is the use of intervening if you only make the situation worse? Wouldn't it be better to let people decide for themselves when they have had enough of tyranny and liberate themselves? The idea that we must help liberate people from tyranny is in principle noble, but in practice, it results in the enslavement of the very people we were supposedly trying to liberate. It is time we saw through the lie that war could ever bring freedom. The people who benefit from war have manipulated the valid desire to help on the part of their citizens to start wars in other countries. We need to hold our leaders accountable for how exactly they intervene in other countries on our behalf.

Are there other, peaceful ways to help bring freedom to people under tyranny? Naturally, there are and these are the options that should be explored. War should never be on the table when thinking about freedom because the two cannot coexist. It is just a question of common sense and the reason this common sense is not commonly applied is because of the people who stand to benefit from endless wars. Why do people accept tyranny in the first place? It is because they don't know any better. They do not have a vision of how different their lives could be without the tyrant. The way to liberate them from tyranny is by raising their awareness. Helping people understand that there is a better way to live is the way to gradually help them throw off the chains of tyranny. The irony is that when the misguided efforts to bring freedom through warfare backfire, it impacts the very people who were supposedly trying to help. We have seen the West struggling with the burden of immigration as people flee from their countries and attempt to find refuge in rich nations. And we have seen the brutality with which these immigrants are dealt with, even leaving them to drown in the seas rather than allowing them to enter these rich countries. And the question is, if you do not want these people to enter your country because you consider them inferior, how can you claim to want freedom for them? In order to help them, you need to see them as human beings like yourself. The West needs to realize that we are all interconnected. You cannot go to these faraway lands to start wars thinking that you will not be affected by the events happening there. Where will these people go when their countries are destroyed? They will come to your very doorstep to look for that very freedom and prosperity you claim to want for them.

War on terror

Ever since 9-11 happened more than two decades ago, the world has been embroiled in a so-called "war on terror", which is whereby we make the world a much more dangerous place in the name of fighting terrorism. The war on terror is a fallacy that has affected many countries including my own country Kenya which in 2011 declared war on the terrorist group Al Shabaab. The most famous war on terror is of course the one carried out by the United States and its allies and it has been used as a justification for invading country after country and for setting up hundreds of military bases around the world. The question that begs then is how do you fight terror? The word terror by definition means an intense or overwhelming fear or a violent action designed to cause extreme fear among ordinary people. So, how exactly do you carry out a war on terror? Is it possible to have a war that could eliminate intense fear? How could this be possible when war itself is one of the greatest causes of fear among human beings? The very idea of a war on terror is illogical. Nothing demonstrates this lack of logic more clearly than the results of the war on terror. Ever since the war on terror began, the world has become a much more dangerous place with the very thing we were trying to eliminate becoming even more prevalent. Did Kenya's war on terror produce any positive results? No, because it made the Al Shabaab even more determined to carry out attacks within the country and the group is still active to this day. The countries that were invaded by the United States in its war on terror i.e., Iraq and Afghanistan went on to produce even worse forms of terror in the form of ISIS. This has led to the situation we now find ourselves in globally whereby we are constantly spied on by our governments in the name of gathering information to fight terrorism. It has led to greater cooperation between the giant tech companies and governments which is leading to less and less freedom of expression. It has led to worse and worse forms of spyware technologies being created and sold to governments in an attempt to shut down dissenting voices. It has led to war crimes such as the ones revealed by Julian Assange. No one has been held accountable for these war crimes, just as no one has been held accountable for the civilian killings during the many wars on terror.

When you think critically about the war on terror, what you find hidden behind this noble-sounding idea is the belief that certain lives are more important than others. In other words, when you invade other countries, aren't you doing to them precisely the same thing you are accusing the terrorists of doing? You are terrorizing innocent people in their own countries. What makes it okay for you to terrorize people yet you do not want your own citizens to be terrorized? What makes it okay to punish a whole country for the sins of some of its citizens? What you are saying is that the lives of the people in your country are worth more than the lives of the people in those countries and therefore the death of one person in your country can be paid for by the deaths of many people in these lessor countries. This must surely be the only reason why instead of treating terrorism as a crime and letting the ones who committed the crime pay for it, you go out and punish an entire country by terrorizing them. How very naïve to start wars and think that you can get away with it, that you can bomb people in faraway countries and it won't circle back to you. We are all connected in ways that are not obvious to some people and whatever you do to others, however far away you think they are it will ultimately come back to you. I have already mentioned some of the ways this happens including the immigration crisis that is facing the West as the people displaced by war come to their countries seeking refuge. We have also seen an increase in authoritarianism with the likes of Donald Trump in the United States, Boris Johnson in the UK and others. One of the main reasons these people are getting elected is the very problem of immigration. People in the West wanted leaders who were tough on immigration. We have seen the impact this rise of authoritarianism has had in these countries. The United States saw a decrease in the prestige and respect it previously enjoyed on the world stage. Many people now consider the United States to be a country in decline. We have also seen how this rise in authoritarianism has divided and polarized citizens iso much it is almost destroying the very foundations of democracy. We are also seeing the militarisation of the police emerge in many of these Western countries. All the excess items that were meant for the military are now being taken up by the police and this is how you end up with a police force that is armed to the teeth. This is how you end up with a police force that increasingly views the public as the enemy rather than people to be protected. What is happening in effect is that the karma is finding its way back to the same countries that are carrying out the war on terror. This is an even greater threat to the West than climate change, which is yet another myth that is being used to distract people from the real issues facing the planet. At a time when the world is on the verge of nuclear war, we cannot afford the luxury of being distracted by climate hysteria which is another creation of the global elites.

Chapter 2
Who Benefits from War

"Of course, the people don't want war. Why would some poor slob on a farm want to risk his life in a war when the best that he can get out of it is to come back to his farm in one piece? But after all, it's the leaders of the country who determine the policy and it's always a simple matter to drag the people along, whether it's a democracy, a fascist dictatorship, or a parliament, or a communist dictatorship. Voice or no voice, the people can always be brought to the bidding of the leaders. That is easy. All you have to do is tell them they are being attacked and denounce the pacifists for lack of patriotism and exposing the country to greater danger. It works the same way in any country."

Herman Goering at the Nuremberg trials

The one thing that is indisputable about war is that it is one of the most harmful activities we have on this planet. Nobody ever truly wants war because the destruction of lives and property that takes place during war goes against human nature which seeks to preserve life. But as we can see from the above quote attributed to Nazi war criminal Herman Goering, the leaders of a country will always find ways to carry everyone along with them into destructive wars that have no benefit for the people. The question then begs, why do these leaders want to fight wars in the first place? What is it about war that would cause leaders to work so hard to override the basic human instinct to preserve life and get people to agree to war? What causes leaders to come up with fancy arguments like the ones we saw in the previous chapter to justify war? What makes them carry out massive propaganda campaigns to get people to agree to war? What makes them go against the wishes of the people and drag their countries into self-destructive wars? As I write this book, the United States is engaged in dangerous escalations against both Russia and China over issues that could easily be resolved through diplomacy. These are nuclear-armed countries so it doesn't take much to imagine what kind of damage a war between them would cause. Such a war would have the potential to wipe out life on the planet as we know it. And yet the leaders of these countries seem to be oblivious to the catastrophic potential of their careless escalations. It is almost as if the very people entrusted with our safety suffer from schizophrenia and the rest of us are forced to look on in disbelief as they run amok threatening to blow up the planet. The doctrine of mutually assured destruction that is supposed to guarantee level-headedness seems to have been thrown out the window. What are we to make of all this? Why are the leaders behaving this way?

To understand this seemingly schizophrenic behaviour of our leaders, we need to be aware that there is more to the war narrative than meets the eye. The truth about war is that it is an industry and a very lucrative one at that. It is a trillion-dollar industry, one of the most commercially viable ventures for anyone who does not mind killing a few thousand or million people for profit. Some people stand to benefit greatly from war and if we are to understand why we continue to have war on this planet, we must begin with this understanding in mind.

The graph below shows the total military spending of countries with the largest military budgets in the world.

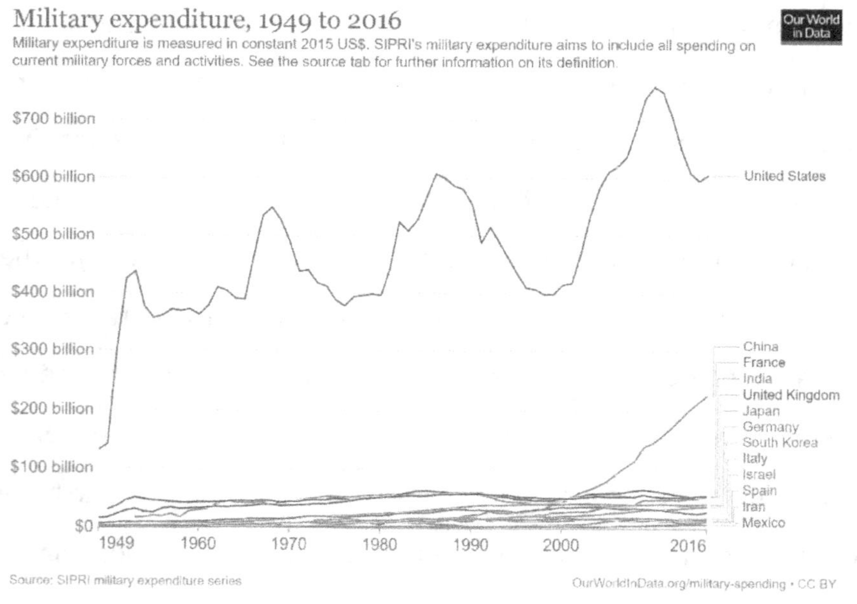

As we can see from the graph, the United States is *by far* the biggest military spender in the world. Is it any wonder then that the United States is involved in so many conflicts around the world? How do you justify spending so much money on your military if there is no war or threat of war? You have to make your citizens believe that they are constantly under threat of attack from people who are jealous of their country. This is the lie that the United States citizens have been fed for a very long time to justify their country spending so much on the military. All those military bases around the world are supposed to defend them from enemies that are supposedly jealous of their "way of life". But the reality is that the United States has become the aggressor that has to constantly look for enemies and create some where none exist to justify all that military spending. From the Middle East to Europe to South America to Africa to Asia, the United States is involved in provocations, escalations and interventions all in a bid to find enemies that would justify their military expenditure.

So, where exactly do all those trillions spent on the military go? The answer to this question will help us understand why it is so difficult to eliminate war on this planet.

Weapons manufacturers

The United States is by far the largest manufacturer of weapons with other major manufacturers being in Europe (United Kingdom, France, Italy and Germany). Other major manufacturers include Japan, Russia and China. The companies producing weapons are valued at billions of dollars. It doesn't take a genius to see that all these weapons have to go somewhere otherwise these industries would not continue to exist. If there were no wars on the planet, these weapons manufacturers would instantly be out of business.

Isn't it ironic that the countries that shout the loudest about human rights are the same ones that produce most of the weapons on the planet? How can they talk about human rights while at the same time manufacturing the weapons that are used in the murder of people around the world? How do these countries justify this hypocrisy? How can we ever hope to live in a peaceful world if these countries continue flooding the world with weapons? When we hear about billion-dollar sales of weapons to countries around the world supplied by these same Western countries that present themselves as morally upright, what are we supposed to think? For example, the United States has been supplying the UAE with billions of dollars worth of weapons, and we all know that these weapons are being used against Yemen. These same Western countries are now falling over themselves to supply Ukraine with weapons, yet they claim to support a diplomatic resolution to the "crisis" between Ukraine and Russia. The hypocrisy is just sickening.

The only way war will ever end on this planet is for these countries to stop producing weapons. As long as these immoral weapons manufacturers are allowed to continue existing, they will continue lobbying their governments for larger and larger military budgets. As long as people are benefitting from the sale of weapons, we will always have wars being fought and the threat of war hanging over our heads. Money that could be used to eliminate poverty and hunger on the planet and give people a better life is instead wasted on the purchase of weapons. When are we going to see through this irony and say enough is enough? The manufacture of weapons should be banned with immediate effect.

While we're on the subject of weapons, let us talk about nuclear weapons. Currently, there are five recognized nuclear-armed countries (United States, United Kingdom, France, China and Russia) and four unofficial nuclear-armed countries (Israel, India, Pakistan and North Korea). The question we need to ask ourselves is why we still allow countries to have nuclear weapons when we already know the destructive capability of these weapons. Why do these countries continue to hold the whole world at ransom with their stockpiles? The idea that some nations are responsible enough to be allowed to hold nuclear weapons evaporated when we saw the irresponsible behaviour of former United States President Donald Trump. I'm sure we all remember with horror the war of words between North Korean leader Kim Jong Un and President Trump. This just exposed the lie that some countries are responsible enough to hold nuclear weapons. The reality is that no country should be allowed to have nuclear weapons whether officially or unofficially. The United Nations Treaty on the Prohibition of Nuclear Weapons (TPNW) came into force on 22nd January 2021, a historic event that was unfortunately not covered by the mainstream media. The world needs to put pressure on the nine nuclear countries to comply with this treaty and get rid of their nuclear weapons so that we can all live without the threat of the imminent destruction of our planet.

Private contractors / Entrepreneurs

The war in Afghanistan cost 2.313 trillion dollars over a period of twenty years or 300 million a day. Where was all this money going? Apart from the purchase of weapons, the military also spends substantial amounts on supplies that keep soldiers on the ground fighting a war. These include food, water, fuel, uniforms, communications equipment, medical supplies, etc. These items have to be supplied by someone and this is where entrepreneurial individuals come in. Companies that supply the military make billions of dollars and if you factor in corruption and inflated costs, the military becomes virtually a gold mine for those who manage to win supply contracts. No wonder no one wants this gravy train to end. All they have to do is not think too much about the consequences of their actions or all the people that get killed. The unfortunate side effect of so much money being allocated to a meaningless activity like war is that it becomes nothing more than a conduit for those in powerful positions to make a lot of money without too much oversight. After all, what metrics would you use to measure the success of the military? Is it the number of people killed? Is it the bullets fired or the bombs dropped? Is it how many buildings have been destroyed? How do you set targets for the military? Do you ensure they fight a war every so often to justify the amount of money allocated to them? The best approach is not to have too much oversight because a lot of uncomfortable questions will inevitably arise. A lot of money released without oversight leads to meaningless activities that are a waste of taxpayer money. By the time audits are carried out, it is often too late as we saw in the case of the Afghanistan war. War is too profitable a venture to expect that the people behind this insanity will stop of their own accord.

Another type of military contractor who makes a killing from war – no pun intended - is the private security contractor or private security companies that provide security in conflict zones. The irony of needing a private security company to protect the military during a war is completely lost on those who consider this a good idea. If your military is made up of well-trained and well-equipped soldiers, why would you need a private security company to protect them? This is just one of the many ironies and contradictions of war and as soon as one starts looking closely at the subject, the lack of logic becomes glaringly obvious. A good example of such security contractors is the infamous Blackwater security company which not only made billions from providing security in Iraq but was also involved in the murder of "innocent" civilians at the Nisour Square in Baghdad. This scandal resulted in the conviction of four Blackwater employees who were later released by former President Donald Trump. Apparently, it is okay to kill people if you are in the military. And what is this idea of categorizing some lives as innocent? Isn't this just another ploy used to justify the murder of human beings by labelling some of them innocent therefore not deserving of death, meaning that others are guilty and therefore deserve death? Who decides who is or isn't innocent or who is or isn't deserving of death? No wonder the four Blackwater employees were released because, at the end of the day, they were doing exactly what they were there to do which was to kill people. Convicting them while not convicting every other soldier involved in war would be an act of hypocrisy. This brings us to the so-called "rules of war", an idea that has become widely accepted. According to this lie, some rules should be observed during war and so long as these rules are observed, then the war is acceptable. One of these rules is that civilian casualties should be minimized or avoided but the deaths of soldiers are acceptable. This rule causes us to minimize the deaths of soldiers who are also human beings that lose their lives on the battle field. All lives are precious and trying to categorize them into civilian and military is a manipulation that tries to make us comfortable with the idea of the senseless slaughter of the young men and women who lose their lives in war. These so-called international rules of war should be abolished and the only international rule of war that should exist is that there should be no war.

Soldiers and other military employees

Governments spend a big chunk of their military budgets on salaries and benefits for soldiers, and when you factor in the war veterans who continue to receive some benefits, the amount needed to pay these people is huge. To attract people into the military, many incentives have to be provided. These include good pay, medical cover, training and hardship allowances. This has made the military a very lucrative career and many young people are willing to risk injury to themselves to join the military. In Africa, countries that cooperate with the United States in their war on terror such as Kenya receive quite some funding as part of this cooperation. This means that soldiers who are sent out to fight as part of this cooperation receive many times what they would normally receive in their normal duties. Other workers who benefit directly from the war industry include translators, cleaners, cooks, drivers, servers and technicians. These could be locals but are more often people from other parts of the world and this is for a very practical reason. Having outsiders provide services during war guarantees that they feel no oneness with the people they are there to fight and this ensures they do not empathize with them. This was an expensive lesson that the United States army learnt while training the local Afghanistan army. Every once in a while, one of the trainees would suddenly turn on his American counterparts and attack them. This became so bad that the American military had to start outsourcing the training of the Afghanistan army.

Billions of dollars are spent rebuilding cities after they are destroyed through bombings and many workers and supplies are needed to do this. It is difficult to understand the rationale behind rebuilding a city after destroying it. Is it that the invading force does not want the images of destruction to reach the world? Is it that they want to create a positive image for the locals after bombing them? Or is it simply one of the ploys used to release billions of dollars towards the "war effort"? It is not clear why this happens; what is clear is that this is another avenue for the expenditure of billions of dollars during war. Naturally, this goes with a lot of wastage and fraud as would be expected when billions of dollars are spent without oversight.

Governments spend a huge part of their countries' GDP on their militaries even without any war to justify this expenditure. For some strange reason, having a military that is in a constant state of readiness for war has become a necessity in the modern world. This mindset is prevalent especially in the West with their huge expenditures on their militaries, but this is becoming the norm throughout the world with bodies such as NATO and the U.S. Department of Defense regional commands propagating this mindset. Instead of spending on healthcare, education, food and housing for their citizens, governments everywhere seem to prioritize the military. The question is, how did we arrive at a point where everyone lives in fear of being attacked necessitating militaries that are ready to go to war at a moment's notice? Is this threat real or imagined? Where did this mindset come from? Imagine if all this money could be used to improve the lives of citizens, how much better off would we be as humanity?

Does it make sense that in the 21st century humanity is still holding on to a primitive, war-like mentality in which safety and security are in constant threat? Isn't it time we moved on to the next level on

Maslow's hierarchy of needs whereby we now start meeting higher needs? How will these needs be met? When all of us start to see ourselves as citizens of planet earth and transcend the idea that we are different from each other. By loving each other enough to care about our brothers and sisters in other parts of the world. As long as we continue seeing people in other parts of the world as different from us, we will always find justification to treat them in ways we would never treat those we see as being like us. As long as we see others as different from us and less than us, we will not be able to feel their pain, which allows us to give consent to our governments to continue bombing and attacking them. If we saw them as our brothers and sisters, nothing could ever justify killing them no matter what our leaders told us.

Are bodies such as NATO or the U.S. Department of Defense regional commands like AFRICOM still relevant today or is it time we moved on from this warlike mentality? Why do we need to live in a world in which readiness for war is a necessity? Isn't it time we abolished not only such bodies but also the militaries we hold on to so dearly and which do not serve any purpose other than draining our resources? We as citizens of the planet need to question some of these ideas that have been carried over from ages past that are no longer relevant today. We need to demand that our governments abolish the militaries because we are ready to move on to a new, 21st-century mindset. As long as we have militaries, we need to have enemies otherwise why do we need the military? And if you see others as enemies, any time you have an issue with them the first thing you will think about is fighting them. When you have no military, you have no option other than to sit down with your neighbours and talk to them.

Some among us who have never questioned why we need to have militaries will be surprised to learn that there are countries today that have no militaries. Countries like Costa Rica, Panama, Haiti and Iceland have no military and this is an example that the rest of us should follow. The assumption that every country must have a military is challenged by these countries that do not have standing militaries. We do not need to spend so much of our country's resources on primitive practices that have no benefit whatsoever to us. Having a standing military does not benefit the citizens, it only benefits the leaders and those who make money off the secret expenditures of the military. Having a standing military only encourages us to respond militarily even when diplomacy would do. The United States is currently on a path of self-destruction because of its massive expenditure on the military even while the standard of living of the average American goes down.   To justify such massive expenditures, the country must constantly look for enemies both real and imagined. Sooner or later, it will meet an enemy that cannot be bullied and that will be the beginning of the end. The best option for the United States is to use its massive influence to promote the peaceful coexistence of humanity. They need to come out of that primitive, warlike mentality and get over the idea that Americans are exceptional. Americans need to learn to co-exist with others not as superiors but as equals. They should use their immense wealth to help lift the planet out of poverty, hunger and disease and then they wouldn't have to worry so much about closing off their borders to keep immigrants out.

Global elites

Global elites are people who see themselves as the leaders of this planet. These are the very rich and powerful individuals who own most of the wealth on the planet, also known as the 1%. They consider themselves superior to the rest of humanity and see themselves as the ones running the world. They see themselves as having the absolute right to rule the planet and decide what happens on a global scale. They do not see themselves as belonging to any one country but see themselves as having the right to do whatever they want in any part of the world. These people are behind many of the wars we have on the planet because they are constantly involved in geopolitical manoeuvres that in their delusional minds mean they are running the world. They feel that they have the right to decide what happens in any part of the world and they do not stand for anything or anyone standing in their way. Any time they encounter resistance from a country in their quest to plunder the country's wealth or natural resources, they resort to aggressive manoeuvres such as regime change, usually done under the pretext of supporting human rights. This is not a secret anymore and the world is slowly waking up to their malign activities. Suffice it to say that any time we hear of unrest in various parts of the world, there is more to the story than meets the eye. In their quest for global dominance, these people will stop at nothing. Their immense wealth and influence allow them to operate behind the scenes, influencing many of the activities we see happening on the world stage.

This desire for global dominance by the elites can be seen for example in the United States' national security doctrine of full-spectrum dominance. This doctrine is responsible for the almost maniacal activities of the United States on the world stage. The idea that one country should dominate the world using its military might is an idea that could only have been dreamt of by a delusional group of elites. This is the reason why the United States has set up military bases in every corner of the planet and is wasting its resources in the quest for global hegemony. Their delusional pursuit of global dominance has blinded them to the fact that they are destroying their nation in the process. This very idea of global dominance is what led Britain to conquer most of the world in the past and we all know how that ended. It is an impossible quest. What we learnt from Britain is that it takes increasing levels of brutality to maintain such a system and it cannot be maintained indefinitely because people will never accept to remain in slavery forever. The United States would do well to learn from Britain's failure in its quest for supremacy. This pursuit of full-spectrum dominance, this delusion created by the globalists will only lead them down a path of self-destruction. By the time the globalists are done, the world will no longer recognize the United States that used to talk about human rights and democracy. Somewhere along the way, they will lose sight of what they were fighting for and become increasingly brutal in their attempt to subdue the planet. They need to stop and ask what price they are willing to pay for their impossible quest for global dominance.

Politicians

The decision to go to war is made ultimately by politicians, so the question is how they benefit from war. It is said that the best way to distract an electorate from domestic problems is to start a war. Politicians use this tactic to distract people by shifting attention away from domestic problems and uniting them to face a common enemy. This just goes to show the kind of people we have in positions of power, people who would send their countrymen off to war just to save their political careers. This is clear proof that many of the people in power are psychopaths. No wonder our planet is in such a mess if life-and-death decisions are being made by people who have no empathy and no conscience.

We know for a fact that politicians are attracted to careers in politics because they offer them power and allow them to feel superior to others. Bullying other countries with the threat of war is a favourite pastime of some leaders, especially in NATO and the United States. Time and time again, politicians talk big and threaten consequences if they don't have their way. We see this today with NATO and the United States threatening consequences on one side and their Russian counterparts threatening even more dire consequences on the other side. These people relish the feeling of power that their militaries and nuclear weapons afford them. The irresponsible behaviour of those who claim to be world leaders is horrifying and it is leading the world closer and closer to nuclear annihilation. As the United States begins its descent into oblivion and other world powers emerge, it is becoming almost a rogue nation in its desire to prove that it is still the most powerful nation on earth.

Another way politicians benefit from war is by being part of the gravy train that is the war industry. Weapons manufacturers spend large sums of money lobbying for laws and policies that favour them. Politicians use their positions of influence to ensure these laws are passed and in return, they receive large contributions to their campaign chests. It's a question of scratch my back and I scratch yours. Millions of dollars end up in politicians' pockets in this way. And let us not forget the revolving door that leads from politics straight into cushy lobbying jobs for politicians once they leave politics. With the contacts and relationships made during their time in politics, a lobbying career becomes the perfect fall-back plan for them. Let us also not forget the jobs that are created by weapons manufacturers. Politicians are some of the biggest supporters of weapons manufacturers because of the jobs created for their electorates. Who cares about the people who will be on the receiving end of the weapons that are manufactured?

Sociopaths

Anyone who has watched the revealing video posted on Wikileaks by Julian Assange will immediately understand why he is being relentlessly pursued by the United States. The video shows a crime against humanity in progress, the brutal killing of helpless civilians by military men. The most shocking part of this video is witnessing the pure bloodthirst of those committing the crime. The level of excitement when the victims come within shooting range is almost palpable. Getting a front-row view of how killing occurs during a war is one of the most disturbing things a person could ever have the misfortune of witnessing. Any notion that wars are a necessity meant to achieve good is dispelled when one sees the reality on the ground. The obvious enjoyment the soldiers get from what they are doing is chilling.

I am not saying that everyone in the military is a sociopath intent on committing murder. Some in the military are simply good people, manipulated into joining the military through the narrative of protecting their country. Once such people experience the reality of war, they come back traumatized, leading many of them to commit suicide or experience severe post-traumatic stress disorder (PTSD). These are the majority of people in the military. I believe though that a portion of the military is made up of people who have no problem with killing. A career in the military offers them the opportunity to indulge this bloodthirst *and* get paid for it.

A close study of human history shows that human beings are not violent by nature. During the hunter/gatherer phase of our existence, there is no evidence that human beings engaged in war against each other. But once humans started settling down during the agricultural phase of our existence, evidence shows that this is when war started becoming a part of our culture. One theory suggests that as people started settling down and populations increased, the sociopaths among them who normally range between 1-4% of the population started increasing in number and were more likely to find each other and organise themselves into groups that could then start causing trouble in the community. This is how war started among human beings and we are still suffering at the hands of sociopaths to this day. With their characteristic aggression and lack of conscience, it would make sense to assume that many positions in the military are held by sociopaths. As long as they are the ones in decision-making positions, we will always have war as diplomacy is not in the vocabulary of these people.

Who does *not* benefit from war

There is one concept human beings love to deny and it is called karma. What goes around comes around. The more a country fights wars and exports violence to other countries, the more this violence comes back to haunt them. The illusion many countries seem to be under especially in the West is that they can export violence to faraway places and they will be fine so long as the wars are fought in other countries. This idea has been turned into an art form with drone warfare. This demonstrates a clear lack of understanding of how the world works. The United States is currently the single largest exporter of violence on the planet with military bases all over the planet, billions in weapons sold to other countries and coups and regime changes organised by the CIA. We are now seeing the United States start to reap what they have been sowing with the violence coming back in the form of the militarisation of the police. The very violence they are exporting to other countries is being turned inward in the form of a brutal police force. It is not just the police force that is becoming violent, ordinary Americans are also buying guns and killing each other in unprecedented numbers. We could say that the chickens have come home to roost as the violence takes hold in their society. How can this be reversed? By Americans standing up to their government and saying no to violence and instead becoming leaders in diplomacy and peace building. Unless we understand that we are interconnected as human beings, we will continue taking actions against each other thinking that we can escape the consequences of our actions, but this is merely an illusion. The law of karma will always catch up with us to teach us the lessons we need to learn about oneness.

We all know about the destruction of lives and property through war but what no one tells us is that this destruction does not only affect the present generation, it affects even future generations. When we talk about the trillions that are used to fund wars, what is left out of the equation is that this money is borrowed money. It is paid for by current generations and it continues to be paid for by future generations. What kind of injustice is this, to saddle future generations with debts incurred for the destruction of lives? When leaders of a country decide to start wars, do they tell their citizens that their children and their children's children will still be paying the debts years later? I guess this is the small print that no one bothers to read and our leaders know this very well. This is the ultimate form of evil, to not only kill present generations but to saddle future generations with the bill.

We need to understand that the whole planet is harmed by war not just the parts of the planet where the wars are fought. War pulls everything downward and the entire planet is dragged down whether we consciously realise it or not. War is a consciousness in which we refuse to see our oneness with each other and feel that we can treat others any way we want and get away with it. This consciousness pulls the whole planet down and keeps it down. If we don't see others as our brothers and sisters, we allow injustice to fester in our midst with a few living in abundance while many wallow in poverty. If we can overcome this consciousness and start seeing others as our brothers and sisters, we will not allow some to live in poverty while others live in plenty. Once we overcome the consciousness of being separate, our eyes will be opened to the injustices and inequality in the world and we can then start addressing them. Overcoming the consciousness of war is the first step toward raising this planet to its potential to provide for the needs of every individual. It is the first step towards demanding a life of dignity for every human being on the planet. It will be the first

step towards truly manifesting the consciousness of oneness on this

planet.

Chapter 3
The Mainstream Media

The media is referred to as the fourth estate and there's a very good reason for this. The term refers to the power and influence of the press which is comparable to the other three arms of government i.e., the legislature, the executive and the judiciary. In democratic countries, the media is supposed to check the other arms of government by keeping people informed and exposing any underhand activities of the government. Because of this, people regard the media as a trustworthy institution, an institution that is on the side of the people and that prevents the excesses of the government. Naturally, the powers that be cannot allow such a powerful institution to become a perpetual thorn in their flesh. Therefore, many governments in many parts of the world are engaged in perpetual wars with the media and journalists, doing everything in their power to prevent the media from doing the important work of acting as their watchdogs. However, we need to understand that the powerful do not always choose to fight the media in overt and aggressive ways. What they do especially in democratic countries is to co-opt the media and slowly turn it into an institution that works for them rather than against them. While autocratic countries prefer to wage endless wars against the media, democratic countries prefer to give the impression of a free and fair media while in reality using the media as nothing more than a mouthpiece in service of the rich and powerful. At the end of the day, the elites get their way meaning they get to do whatever they want while the common man is none the wiser. How do they achieve this? Through outright ownership of media houses or through strong-arming the media into doing their bidding, as we have seen with the major digital platforms that are becoming more and more aligned with the official narrative of the elites. We have seen censorship becoming normalized as digital platforms work to silence any voices that say anything other than the approved narratives. We saw this trend during the Covid-19 pandemic when it became impossible to voice any opinion that did not agree with the official narrative. It didn't take long for this trend to be applied to other topics such as the Russia-Ukraine war. Anyone who blindly accepts that the freedom of speech should be curtailed for whatever reason, be it the pandemic or the war in Ukraine does not understand how the powerful operate. The powerful use narratives to control the masses. They lie and deceive constantly to achieve their ends. We must also understand that their end goal is to take away all our freedoms. Today it is the freedom of speech that is taken away, tomorrow it is the freedom of movement and the day after it will be the right to life itself. That is why we should never accept that our freedoms should be taken away for any reason. Once gone, they are unlikely to ever come back again.

With regard to war, the media is a powerful tool that the elites use in getting the masses to support wars that neither benefit nor serve them in any way. The media is weaponized against the masses and slowly without anyone realizing it, the powerful entrench their worldview on an unsuspecting world. People become so deceived, so emersed in the false narratives of the powerful that we never see clearly what they are doing. Without understanding what is happening, we slowly become passive pawns in a game that is of the elites, by the elites and for the elites. In this chapter, we will look at the role of the media in the war industry.

Propaganda

"This is the secret of propaganda: Those who are to be persuaded by it should be completely immersed in the ideas of the propaganda, without ever noticing that they are being immersed in it."

Joseph Goebbels

The media is a lethal weapon for anyone interested in spreading war propaganda and no one understood this better than Joseph Goebbels, the propaganda minister of the Nazi regime. Propaganda can be defined as information, ideas, opinions, or images, often only giving one part of an argument, that is broadcast, published, or in some other way spread to influence people's opinions. How did the Nazis succeed in getting the Germans to go along with an ideology so immoral that it led to the murder of millions of people across Europe? Through the use of propaganda. The Nazis had a very good understanding of human psychology and they used it very effectively, to the detriment of humanity. They understood that if you take an idea, no matter how outlandish and repeat it endlessly, people will eventually accept it as the truth. Today, the media is still being used against us in subtle ways that we can't even see.   As stated in Goebbels' quote above, propaganda is most effective when people are unaware that they are being subjected to it. If we thought that propaganda ended when the Nazis lost power, we are completely wrong. There is a very good reason why the elites work so hard to control the media. It is because this is the only way to get the masses to do whatever they want without them knowing that they are being controlled.   Our understanding of what is happening in the world in general and our understanding of war, in particular, is shaped by what the media tells us. Not only do they tell us what is happening, but they shape the way we think about what is happening.

Propaganda during the Russia-Ukraine War

"Propaganda must facilitate the displacement of aggression by specifying the targets for hatred."

Joseph Goebbels

On 24 February 2022, Russia invaded Ukraine. In their rush to control the narrative, the West went all out to ensure that their version of events dominated the airwaves. What seemed to be a coordinated message was churned out 24/7 to the world through the mainstream media which painted Russia as the aggressor and the West as the innocent bystanders doing everything possible to stop Russia's aggression. The almost non-stop coverage of the Covid-19 pandemic which the world had endured for almost two years abruptly ended, and the mainstream media shifted its attention to the Russia-Ukraine war. The repetitive use of the words "aggressor" and "unprovoked" to describe Russia was a clever use of Goebbels' idea described in the quote above. The aggressor had to be identified so that the world would know where to direct its anger and hatred. There was a systematic attempt to paint the war as completely unprovoked, the result of a mad, isolated President Putin lashing out in an attempt to end democracy in Ukraine and fulfil his imperial ambitions.

Those of us who understand how the world works know that wars do not just happen. There is always more to the story than meets the eye. If we just take whatever we are told without taking the time to analyse it, we become victims of a propaganda war that is fought in tandem with the real war. We know that the West is not the innocent bystander it makes itself out to be. They spent years goading Russia into this war and finally, they succeeded. Through the NATO strategy of relentless expansion, Russia was finally provoked into going to war, which is arguably what the West wanted and had been working towards all along. The point I'm trying to make is that there are no innocent parties here. We need to always keep in mind that some people benefit from war and they are always working in the background to provoke wars. When wars finally break out, their role is hidden from view. We saw this happen right in front of our eyes with the Russia-Ukraine war. For years, analysts had warned that a dangerous situation was unfolding around Ukraine but when the war finally broke out, the media tried to get us to believe that the war was "unprovoked".

Something else we saw happen very quickly was the censorship of the media. The European Union banned Russian news channels like Sputnik and RT. These news channels provide a different perspective than the one offered by the West, and so they were labelled as misinformation. Misinformation was redefined to mean anything that does not agree with the powers that be. Digital platforms like Facebook, Twitter and YouTube used their powerful algorithms to bury anything that was not pro-West. Not to be left behind, Russia banned the use of words like "invasion", "attack" or "declaration of war" on all digital platforms. They claimed that this was not a war but a "special military operation". How do you attack another country and cause millions to flee their homes and still get to decide that it is not a war? This was propaganda at its best. Powerful people understand the power of the media in shaping how we think about what is happening around us.

Normalising War

Why is it that human beings have an almost universal acceptance of the inevitability of war? We seem to have accepted the idea that war is a fact of life and that human beings will always be inclined to fight each other. But this idea is not based on any observable fact. For long periods during our earliest history, human beings were able to co-exist peacefully with each other. Even today, there are many parts of the world where people co-exist peacefully. Instead of studying these communities to learn how they do it, we continue to mindlessly accept the false idea that war is an inevitable part of human existence. We rely on the media to tell us what is happening during war since we have no other way of knowing what is happening on the battlefield, and this makes us vulnerable to whatever narrative the media decides to feed us. But it doesn't stop there. The media also tells us *how* to think about what is happening which is why they invite experts to analyse the events. The "experts" look at the events from every possible angle, but the one thing they never do is question the status quo. They never look at the issue from a moral perspective; instead, they make it appear almost normal for people to kill each other. The media sets aside morality when it comes to war and only considers it from an amoral perspective where the higher human ideals do not apply. When governments send weapons to the war zone, the media applauds this almost as if they have no idea what the weapons are being used for. Why pretend to be sad about the death toll while celebrating the fact that governments are sending weapons to the war zone? What exactly did they think those weapons were going to be used for? The media only looks at war from a simplistic perspective such as which army is stronger, which weapons are being used by each side, who is likely to win the war, etc. In other words, they give the appearance of having a very lively debate about war, but in reality, the debate is confined to a very narrow, limited scope. The media never admits the existence of any other worldview apart from one in which war is normal and inevitable.

As an example, when the Russia-Ukraine war started, the Dalai Lama spoke out against the war. Part of his statement was as follows:

"War is out-dated – non-violence is the only way. We need to develop a sense of the oneness of humanity by considering other human beings as brothers and sisters. This is how we will build a more peaceful world."

The mainstream media barely reported on this. The mainstream media seems completely disinterested in any other narrative apart from their own. They never or rarely seek the opinion of religious leaders or anti-war organisations or anyone who would give people a different view of war. We never hear from people like the Dalai Lama who would help humanity start to wake up from the nightmare of perpetual war by questioning the very ideology of war. When Germany took the moral stand of not sending weapons to Ukraine, they were mocked by the mainstream media and it didn't take long for Germany to capitulate. This was quickly applauded as the right thing to do. Germany, the country that was responsible for starting World War II failed in its duty to take a moral stand against the war in Ukraine and therefore missed the opportunity to be a voice of reason. They missed the opportunity to take a moral stand like they did during the immigration crisis during which they agreed to take in a million immigrants while the rest of Europe did their best to keep the immigrants out.

If the media was at all interested in ending wars on the planet, they would take a moral stand by doing everything within their power to de-escalate tensions. We have to remember that a problem cannot be solved at the same level of consciousness at which it was created. You cannot solve the problem of war by trying to decide which side is justified or which side is on the right. This is the level of consciousness where wars are created. The only way to solve the problem is by looking at it from a higher perspective. The media should remain neutral and speak out against war rather than engage in the same arguments that caused the war. In a war, no side is right because both sides are committing atrocities against each other. It doesn't matter who started the war in the first place; once a war starts then both sides lose the moral high ground. It makes no sense to argue that one side has the moral high ground because the other side started the war. The correct stance is that both sides need to stop fighting and go to the negotiating table. This tendency of the media to take sides keeps people lost in endless arguments that do nothing to bring about peace. The media should amplify voices of reason and shut out voices that call for violence and escalation. If the media was truly a voice for good, they would never accept war as normal and they would use their power to help end wars.

Sanitising war

One thing we notice about the way the media reports on war is that we are rarely shown the true horrors of war. It is almost as if a shroud of darkness covers the topic so that people don't quite grasp the sheer evil and depravity of it. Deaths are reduced to mere numbers which remove the emotional aspect of it. The result is that people become numb and go about their lives without being moved by the horror that is unfolding in other parts of the world. There seems to be an almost unspoken agreement within the media that horrific scenes of war should never be shown on our screens. At first glance, it would appear as if this is a responsible stance on the part of the media, but the reality is that our screens are already full of scenes of violence, especially from the entertainment media. It thus becomes difficult to believe that the reason we don't see the true horrors of war is because of responsible journalism. When we do get to see images of war, what we see are identical images on all the mainstream media, almost as if they all come from the same source. The images are usually non-alarming - immigrants trying to flee to a neighbouring country or fighter jets taking off or a few buildings destroyed. Nothing too alarming, nothing that would make people recoil in horror at the atrocities being committed in other countries. The reality behind this very uniform way of reporting is that most of the news we consume today is produced by international news agencies such as the Associated Press (AP), Reuters and Agence France-Presse (AFP). Due to the enormous expense of having journalists stationed all over the world, most media houses today choose instead to purchase news from these news agencies. It is therefore not difficult to see how the global elites who have an interest in controlling how we perceive the world would control the information we consume. All they have to do is gain control of the news agencies and skew the news in whatever direction they prefer. This is the main reason why it almost doesn't matter which mainstream media channel you tune into; you will still receive more or less the same coverage. When it comes to war, this model ensures we receive sanitized reports that do not alarm us and that push the narrative that is preferred by the global elites.

What would happen if the media started showing the true horrors of war? Think about how the world reacted to the images of the second world war. When people saw what was done to Jews in concentration camps and the horrors of the atomic bombs that were dropped on Hiroshima and Nagasaki, people reacted with so much horror that it made the world vow "never again". Anyone who saw those images could not help but feel that such a thing should never be allowed to happen again. But what has happened since those days? We don't see the true horrors of war anymore. Deaths are nothing more than statistics that mean nothing to us. As the brutal dictator, Joseph Stalin once commented, "A single death is a tragedy; a million deaths is a statistic." By hiding the true horrors of war, we have lost the natural reaction that war should be avoided at all costs. This is why people today are making reckless calls for a war between nuclear-armed countries. We have forgotten what war means and we don't seem to have the ability to imagine the horrors of a nuclear war. The media has slowly hidden the understanding that nuclear war would mean the end of humanity, not just from the explosions but from the ensuing nuclear winter. This sanitizing of war is the reason the world is slowly sleepwalking towards nuclear war.

Minimising war

The way the media treats the outbreak of war makes it appear as if it is just another event in a series of events happening on the planet. The fact that the world is engaged in so many wars is not treated as something that should concern anyone. War is made to appear as if it is no big deal, especially if it happens to be in places like the Middle East or Africa where it is deemed acceptable and normal for war to take place. Because of this, people just tune out whenever they hear of yet another war breaking out in these places. Wars in these places are looked at in a simplistic way using the same talking points about terrorism and extremism in the Middle East or savagery, clannism and tribalism in Africa. This tendency by the media to minimize war is brought into sharp focus when we compare how the media reacted to the Russia-Ukraine war versus how it reacts to wars in the Middle East or Africa. There was horror and sadness for European, blonde, blue-eyed people being forced to flee their homes. No one shed any tears for the people of Afghanistan, Iraq, Syria, Libya or Yemen. In other words, there is nothing wrong with Africans or Arabs fleeing their homes, but it is unacceptable for Europeans to suffer the same indignity. This is how wars in these parts of the world are minimized because people have been programmed to expect wars in these places.

Another thing we see is that the standards for what is deemed acceptable in the media have become so low that things that would have been considered extreme not so long ago are now considered normal. It is normal these days for leaders to call for nuclear war in the mainstream media. There were aggressive calls in the media for the West to enforce a no-fly zone over Ukraine without explaining clearly what this would mean. Anyone with even a bit of common sense understands that if the West enforced a no-fly zone over Ukraine, it would lead to a confrontation between nuclear-armed countries. How did we move from the horrors of Hiroshima and Nagasaki that caused the world to say "never again" to politicians calling for nuclear war? The idea of nuclear war has become so minimized that it is made to sound like it would be worth it just to stop Russia. If anything, the West is made to look cowardly for not doing everything within its power to intervene. If everyone on the planet is not horrified by this, it is because our senses have become so dulled and war so minimized that we don't even understand the danger we are all being placed in.

Is it that the media does not understand its role in inflaming people and pushing them towards violence? Surely in this day and age, everyone understands the danger of an unbalanced media. Everyone understands the power of the media, from its role in the Rwandan genocide to its role in World War II. And yet today we still see "respected" media outlets allowing their platforms to be used to spread despicable ideas while minimizing the horror that these ideas represent. During the Russia-Ukraine war, social media allowed videos to be broadcast giving instructions on how to make Molotov cocktails. Since these were going to be used to kill Russian soldiers who were the bad guys, there was no cause for alarm. In other words, killing human beings is no longer something that people should recoil from but rather something that one can learn online. Can you imagine living in a world in which normal people know how to make Molotov cocktails? This sounds to me like a very undesirable thing. This minimising of war is something we should all be opposed to. We should not allow the media to cause us to slide down a slope into an abyss where morality does not exist. There should be no exceptions that make it right for people to be taught how to kill. Teaching people how to kill takes the idea of the sanctity of life and throws it out the window.

The media has a responsibility to report on war without minimizing its horrors or justifying the actions of any side of the war. They have a responsibility to find out the hidden issues and bring the truth to the world. They have a responsibility to do their part to reduce tensions rather than increase them. They have a responsibility to call for peace and hold leaders accountable. This has always been the role of the media, to shine a light where there is darkness. Unfortunately, we don't see this. What we see is the media taking sides, portraying one side as the devil while the other side is portrayed as the angel that can do no wrong. We see a media that has allowed itself to become a tool for the global elites to spread their agenda, to the detriment of the rest of humanity.

Politicising war

Another strategy the media employs in shaping how we think about war is politicising war, which causes us to lose sight of the bigger picture. Instead of looking at war as a moral issue, every analysis in the media looks at it purely from a political or geopolitical standpoint. The idea that war is evil in and of itself is never addressed. Rather, we are told that there are good wars and there are bad wars. Good wars are those that benefit us in some strategic way while bad wars are those that do not benefit us strategically. This refusal to look at war as an evil that cannot be justified no matter what causes people to get mired in endless political arguments for or against war. Anyone who attempts to stay above the fray and look at war as a moral issue is seen as naïve or simply ignored. The "experts" who give their analyses certainly do not look at war as a moral issue. For them, war is about what benefits the country geopolitically and how best to position the country to win according to their delusional ideas of what winning means.

A good example of how war is politicized can be seen in the Russia-Ukraine war. There was a lot of hysteria in the media about the war, but at no point was the issue looked at from a moral standpoint. Every analysis was about what President Putin wanted to achieve and what his next move would be and whether the West should intervene or not. There were repeated proclamations by the United States that NATO would defend every inch of NATO territory without addressing exactly what that would mean. Ukraine's president Volodymyr Zelensky was hailed as a hero because of his ability to rally the world around Ukraine, but no one talked about the danger in which he placed his country by his refusal to negotiate a peaceful settlement with Russia and his consistent calls for the West to intervene in the war. If Zelensky cared about his country, he would have been willing to negotiate an agreement that would have prevented war in the first place. Only a psychopath would consider it worthwhile for many people to die just to prove a point. If he was a hero, he would not have tried to join NATO, an outdated body whose only purpose is to keep the world in a perpetual state of war. But unfortunately, the media never looks at issues from a moral standpoint. Somehow, they managed to paint someone whose recklessness led his country to war as a hero.

The United States is one of the countries that is most affected by this manipulation of the media which means that every issue is looked at from a political standpoint. In the United States, everything is about the democrats versus the republicans, which essentially pushes people into two opposing camps that can never agree on anything. This very narrow way of looking at the world causes the country to be manipulated into looking at everything as a fight to the death between two opposing sides. People are forced to choose one camp, either democrat or republican with each side having predetermined views on every topic. Rather than seeing people as individuals capable of having complex views on any issue, people are viewed as simpletons capable of looking at issues only from a democrat versus republican standpoint. It then becomes easy to manipulate people by framing every issue as democrat versus republican, conservative versus liberal. When it comes to war, the media uses the same strategy to manipulate people into supporting wars.

The effect of politicising war is that the media becomes complicit by not reporting anything that would cast the government in a bad light. Rather than being a watchdog that holds the government accountable, the media becomes a partner that works hand in hand with the government in ways that hurt the people. For example, with the Russia-Ukraine war, the media could have highlighted the hypocrisy of the West condemning the actions of Russia while being guilty of the same crimes. Instead, the media studiously ignored this fact and thus missed the opportunity to raise public awareness. Instead of pointing out the hypocrisy of Western governments eagerly welcoming Ukrainian refugees while allowing thousands of Syrian and North African refugees to freeze to death or drown in the seas, the media acted as if it has no memory or awareness of these issues. What then is the purpose of the media if not to keep governments accountable? If there is no one to speak out against the evil actions and the hypocrisy of governments, how will governments be pressured into doing the right thing? Traditionally, this has always been the role of the media.

But if the media becomes complicit in the failings of the government and hides things from the people, what hope is there for the people? This could explain why the media went from being one of the most trusted institutions to one of the least trusted institutions today. It is because the media no longer stands for truth but has instead become another arm of the government.

Manufacturing consent

When a government decides to go to war with another country for whatever delusional geostrategic reason they come up with, one of the main hurdles they face is that most people naturally do not want war. Why would anyone in their right mind want wars which result in death and destruction of lives and property? Most human beings are naturally opposed to war and to get them to change their minds and support wars that are of no benefit to them, governments must use media propaganda as their main weapon. To get people to support war, governments must make them feel threatened or afraid of some external enemy. They must whip up people's emotions and cause them to be filled with hatred and fear towards their perceived enemy. They must make people feel that the enemy presents an existential threat to them even though the enemy may be thousands of kilometres away. They must make people give up their natural desire for peace and security and manipulate them into thinking they have to temporarily give these up to deal with an existential threat. They must cause people to feel so fearful of a supposed threat that they willingly consent to any action that reduces or eliminates the threat.

We see this happening time and time again. After the September 11 bombings in America, the hysteria and fear that ensued were used to manufacture consent for wars in Iraq and Afghanistan that should never have happened in the first place. Instead of calming the public and using legal means to address the crimes that were committed, all reason was thrown out the window and war quickly became the only option. Whole countries were made to pay for the crimes of people who did not even hail from those countries. The media certainly played its part in causing and sustaining the hysteria and before anyone knew what was happening, the public had been manipulated into consenting to wars that destroyed whole countries and tied up American resources for decades. We saw this same manipulation during the Russia-Ukraine war when the world rallied behind the West to "defend democracy". Whether there was democracy in Ukraine, to begin with, is debatable but that is not even the point. Why would the West be manipulated into thinking that they needed to be involved in wars that had nothing to do with them? What does the war in Ukraine have to do with Americans and why would they be willing to risk nuclear war to protect Ukraine's democracy? Unfortunately, this kind of manipulation is used to manufacture consent in democratic countries because governments need to at least pretend to get the consent of the people for their wars and they do this by tapping into the primal fears that lie just beneath the surface in most human beings.

Autocratic governments on the other hand do not necessarily need to get people to agree with their actions, but they do need to provide a narrative that keeps people passive, which allows the government to do whatever it wants. Without a narrative that keeps people passive, there would be the risk of people revolting against their governments. We saw this happen in Russia when they invaded Ukraine with the word "war" being replaced by "special military operation" to "demilitarize and denazify" Ukraine. So, although it has all the characteristics of war, no one is allowed to call it a war. The special military operation was also said to be a "humanitarian intervention" for the people of the Donbas region, never mind the fact that it forced millions of Ukrainians to flee from their homes.

Controlling the Narrative

War is an unacceptable evil in and of itself, but it is possible to manipulate people into forgetting this fact and supporting one side or the other. People who ordinarily would never support the mass murder of human beings find themselves looking at things from a distorted perspective in which one side is somehow justified in the war. How is this achieved? Through manipulation of the narrative by the mainstream media. Whoever controls the narrative has already won half the battle and, in this regard, the West surely is the undisputed winner. The West has effectively managed to convince the world that their actions are good and moral, even though when looked at objectively, they are immoral. The West has pushed the idea that their wars are righteous because they are fought to bring freedom and democracy in places that are ruled by tyrants. The West has also managed to paint countries like China and Russia as inherently evil meaning that whatever they do can only be evil. Meanwhile, the West has painted itself as the saviour of humanity, meaning that whatever they do is inherently good and beneficial for the world. This worldview has been so aggressively perpetuated by the media that it has taken a very long time for people to begin seeing through it. How many countries have been invaded by the United States in the name of bringing freedom? Countries like Libya, Iraq, Afghanistan and Syria have all been victims of this false narrative. Once this "freedom" is achieved, these countries are usually much worse than they were before. It has taken a long time for people to start seeing the West for what it is and to start pushing back against this narrative. Unfortunately, most people remain blinded by the false narrative.

One of the most interesting things to watch during the Russia-Ukraine war was the way the United States, apparently without irony, kept saying that no country should be allowed to invade another sovereign state. It just makes one wonder exactly what the United States called their invasion of the above-mentioned countries. Was it an invasion or was it merely an attempt to bring freedom and democracy to the people? Anyone who tries to point out that the actions of the West were just as evil as the actions of Russia is painted as pro-Russia and pro-Putin. This is how the media controls the narrative. Instead of the conversation being about real issues, the conversation becomes an endless back-and-forth that does not address the problem. The other interesting thing to watch was how nations around the world rushed to condemn Russia whereas we never saw the same condemnation of the West. If morality and integrity are the standards by which the actions of a country should be judged, then any country that invades another country should be condemned no matter who they are.

This attempt to control the narrative is of course not confined to the West as we have seen the same thing happening in other countries. Facebook being a pro-West platform is banned in China, North Korea and now Russia. A pro-West narrative is naturally not desirable in communist countries or countries that disagree with the West. In these countries, the government maintains a tight grip on the media which allows them to control the narrative in their countries. This is not to suggest that digital platforms like Facebook are innocent players in the game. Far from it. We saw how Facebook announced that it would temporarily change its hate speech policy to allow hate speech that is directed toward Russia. How such a policy can be justified by anyone is beyond comprehension. That said, people should be allowed to make choices regarding which media they prefer. Banning and censorship only lead in one direction – towards less and less freedom of speech.

Without any standard of truth and integrity guiding their actions, the media becomes complicit in the narrative control that the elites use to deceive the masses. We mentioned in the previous chapter that wars have beneficiaries. How do these people ensure that their presence is hidden so that they continue reaping the benefits of war? Through narrative control. They hide their true motives and sell whatever narrative serves their purpose. War is called a peacekeeping mission or a humanitarian mission. Regime change is called bringing freedom and democracy. Destabilization is called democracy at work. Meanwhile, the real enemies, the global elites who hide behind every conflict on the planet rake in the profits.

Diverting Attention

The media is an important tool when it comes to driving people's attention. We have no way of knowing what is happening in other parts of the world unless we hear about it in the news. This power unfortunately can be used both for good and evil. Once we understand that most of the media is controlled by the elites, it becomes easy to see how this powerful tool can be used to drive our attention towards or away from certain information. This may take the form of censorship which stops us from hearing certain views that do not favour the elite narrative, or it may take the form of simply ignoring certain topics that we do not need to know about. In the context of war, this is what leads to the concept of forgotten wars i.e., wars we never hear about in the media.

How many of us know that there is a war going on in Somalia? Who remembers that several countries including Kenya have been waging a war against terror backed by the United States in Somalia for more than a decade? The media never talks about this. What about the war in Ethiopia? This is quickly fading from our collective memory as the media moves on to other "more important" things. After carrying out a propaganda campaign in which the real story was hidden from the public, the media quickly forgot about the war in Ethiopia. What about the war in Yemen? Do Americans know that their government has been supporting Saudi Arabia by providing the weapons that are used against the people of Yemen? Most likely they do not know this as the media does not focus their attention on this. The only narrative the world gets to hear favours the powers that be. Any narrative that portrays them as anything other than the benevolent saviours of the planet is hidden, never to be talked about except in remote corners of the internet. If the media would honestly focus the attention of the world on all the wars that are taking place on the planet and highlight the role of countries like the United States or France in these wars, then the very false idea the world holds about these countries would quickly evaporate.

During the twenty years that the United States was in Afghanistan, the media never highlighted the fact that the United States was at war with Afghanistan. All I remember reading about were stories about suicide bombers blowing themselves up in marketplaces and mosques. There was no context, no background, nothing except the portrayal of

Afghanis as evil people who for no reason whatsoever felt the need to blow themselves up. It was not until the United States withdrew from Afghanistan in August 2021 that we were reminded that they had been at war with Afghanistan for two decades. This is how the media operates, selectively driving our attention in whichever direction they prefer. No wonder many reporters in the West seem to think that a war in Europe (the Russia-Ukraine war) is an unusual event. The world has for a very long time been painted in such a way that wars only happen in the Middle East and Africa. No one remembers that two world wars were fought in Europe not that long ago.

We saw the power of the media at the start of the Russia-Ukraine war when the narrative shifted from the war itself to the "stand with Ukraine" rallying call. Instead of focusing on the lives that were being destroyed and the pure evil that was unfolding, it became about standing with Ukraine by displaying their flag on one's social media. Every effort was made to paint European countries as overflowing with brotherly love and concern for their besieged neighbour, never mind that just a few weeks prior the media had been awash with stories of Middle Eastern and African immigrants drowning in the seas or freezing to death because no one was willing to take them in. Afterwards, the media quickly shifted our attention to the sanctions that were being slapped on Russia, giving the impression that the whole world was in support of the West in their outrage against Russia. While the bombs were falling and bullets flying, our attention was focused on sending out flag emojis to show solidarity with Ukraine.

What happens when our attention is diverted from the real issues? It prevents us from debating the real issues and keeps us busy with non-issues. The real issues like the immorality of war or the hidden forces behind war are never addressed. We never discuss the bigger questions such as why humanity is headed towards another world war, and why we are devolving when we should be evolving. Why are we still fighting wars in the 21st century? Why do we allow our leaders to lead us to war when the majority of us do not want war? Why is it that the media amplifies the most aggressive voices that call for escalation rather than the voices that call for peace? Why are we not having a more nuanced discussion about why human beings cannot live at peace with each other when this is what we all want deep down?

Chapter 4
The Entertainment Industry

Most of us think of entertainment as a harmless distraction from everyday life, something we do when we have free time. We think of entertainment as something that enables us to relax after a hard day's work or as a way to connect with others. What we may not be aware of is how much the entertainment industry shapes our views about the world we live in. When we sit down to watch a movie or play online games, we mostly set aside our analytical thinking and take in whatever is presented to us without question. When our minds are in this open and receptive state and our analytical thinking is set aside, we become open to suggestions, ideas, programming and even mind-control. We need to understand that our world is controlled by a determined group of elites who desire to control our thoughts, our beliefs and ultimately our actions. What better way to achieve this than by making us believe that what we watch is a harmless distraction that has no bearing whatsoever on what we think or believe? What better way than to make us think that there is no connection between real life and the make-believe world of entertainment? In reality, the divide is not as clear-cut as we would like to believe. While we may not take in everything we watch as the gospel truth, we cannot avoid being influenced by some of it. We cannot dismiss the idea of subliminal messaging, whereby ideas are transmitted into our subconscious minds without our conscious awareness. This kind of messaging influences our thoughts in ways that we cannot even begin to imagine, from advertisers influencing what we buy to politicians influencing how we vote. If we imagine that the elites would resist the temptation to use such a powerful tool to influence us, then we are simply being naïve. Their desire for control of the masses is much too great for them to resist such an obvious and freely available channel.

One aspect of the entertainment industry that has exploded in the last decade or so is the gaming industry. Games are no longer meant only for children but today are targeted towards adults as well. During the Covid-19 pandemic, there was an explosion in online gaming and many people became addicted to gaming. With mobile phones in everyone's hands, gaming has taken off in a big way. Gaming truly is becoming the entertainment of the future, especially with technological advancements that make the gaming experience even more real. With companies like Meta (Facebook) looking to tap into this human desire for distraction by creating an alternate reality in which human beings can completely lose themselves, we shouldn't be surprised if this trend takes on a more nefarious direction. The elites have absolutely no qualms about introducing technological advancements that are harmful to the rest of us so long as they make a lot of money in the process. Since this book is about war, let us examine the role the entertainment industry plays in influencing our ideas and beliefs about war. These ideas and beliefs are the reason we continue to have wars on this planet.

Romanticizing war

Hollywood has a very interesting take on the subject of war. We all know that war is a violent, brutal activity, but the entertainment industry somehow makes it appear romantic, even heroic. Soldiers are depicted as heroes valiantly serving their countries. We are shown scenes of wives lovingly embracing their husbands and mothers tearfully holding on to their sons as they go off to war. Young men solemnly promise to come back home – as if this was in their control – while fathers stoically watch their sons go off to be killed and maimed. No one ever seems to question why young men should be sent off to die in war. Everyone seems to accept that war is necessary if difficult and that one must bravely comply when called upon to defend one's country. This very romanticized view of war is pure brainwashing, meant to manipulate people into thinking about war in a certain way. We are brainwashed into thinking of war as a call of duty which every sensible person gives in to without question. The authorities that send our sons off to war are not to be questioned or defied. Once the call is made to go to war, everything else becomes secondary. Love no longer matters, families no longer matter, feelings no longer matter – nothing matters except fighting the enemy.

As an example of how war is romanticised, think of *The Sound of Music*, one of the most popular movies of all time. The movie was set during the second world war and it somehow manages to weave the themes of love and war into one intertwined whole. This mixing of romance with war serves to portray war in an almost romantic light. The fear and desperation of the Von Trapp family as they try to flee only serve to heighten the romance. Without us realizing it, war becomes inextricably linked with love in our minds and the whole idea takes on a romantic hue. Another good example is the Netflix show *Downton Abbey* which at one point depicts the heroism of an aristocratic family converting their house into a hospital for wounded soldiers. Rather than pointing a spotlight on the inhumanity of the powerful people who make the decisions that send people to be killed in wars, what we see instead is the romanticized image of doctors and nurses working tirelessly to save lives. The same show brings out other themes such as the cowardice of a man who finds a way to avoid going to war, almost as if war is something that everyone should be eager to go to. It is a complete manipulation of reality on the part of the entertainment industry. They pervert the idea of the sanctity of life and make it such that wanting to preserve one's life is a cowardly act. Being reluctant to kill people and experience the horrors of war is depicted as cowardly while being eager to go to war and kill the enemy is depicted as heroic. Young men are brainwashed into believing that they should be eager to give their lives to serve their countries. Parents are brainwashed into believing that they should be willing to send their children off to war. Wives are brainwashed into believing that they should be sad but understanding when their husbands go off to war. This is a complete perversion of the sanctity of life. We should be eager to preserve life not take it. We should do everything in our power to protect our loved ones from the horrors of war, not quietly submit to the elites who send our loved ones to die. No one should have to accept that war is inevitable. It is high time we all refused to give in to the insanity of the elites who demand that we send our young men to die in their useless wars.

Rewriting history

It's been said that history is written by the winners, which means that the version of history we get to hear is the one written by the winners. Therefore, by definition, this version cannot be the full story. The losers in a war also have their version of events, but unfortunately, we never get to hear this version. If a group of people viciously attacks another group of people and takes away their land by force, robs them of their resources and brutally oppresses them, the version of the story we get to hear is that a heroic group of people conquered and subdued the enemy. According to this version, the conquerors are heroes who should be hailed by all and monuments built in their honour. History is full of such stories. We never get to hear of the brutality of the invading armies. We never get to hear about the wealth they stole and carried back to their lands. We never get to know about the hidden motives that drove them to attack in the first place. All we hear about is their courage and heroism. No wonder we have monuments everywhere celebrating the actions of the most brutal people that have ever walked on this planet. It is because they write history to favour themselves.

The entertainment industry plays a very important role in ensuring we only get to hear the version of history that the elites prefer. Most of us have watched movies that portray certain countries or regions in a positive light while others are portrayed in a negative light. These portrayals affect how we think of the world we live in. For example, we have the stereotype of Muslims and Arabs as terrorists who will blow up anything for obscure religious reasons. Westerners on the other hand are portrayed as rational, reasonable people who always act morally. Thus, when they invade a country in the Middle East, it can only be in pursuit of a moral agenda in the face of an immoral, insane enemy who can never be trusted to act rationally. This reinforces the idea of white supremacy that is so entrenched on this planet. We are also familiar with the trope of the savage, illiterate, uncivilized Africans who spend all their time in tribal wars and cannot be trusted to manage their affairs. Westerners are portrayed as the civilizing, Christianising force that came to save Africans from themselves. Thus, their vicious takeover of African land and their brutal oppression of Africans are framed as being good for the Africans. The Westerners are the heroes who brought civilization to the savage Africans. Even today, some Westerners still believe this nonsense because it has been fed to them for so long. Who wants to take a deeper look at history if you have been told over and over that you are the ones who brought civilization to the world? Westerners as a whole are reluctant to look at the reality of their past because they cannot deal with the idea that the rosy picture that was painted about them is nothing but a rewriting of history. To get an idea of just how brainwashed Westerners are, consider the ludicrous debate currently going on about whether the West should return the art that was stolen from West Africans during colonial times. Consider the very arrogant and patronizing attitude of some Westerners who feel that the art should not be returned to Africans because they cannot be trusted to take care of it. How could these people be so lacking in self-awareness that they could come up with such an argument? If the people who created the art cannot be trusted to take care of it, who then can be trusted to take care of it? The people who stole it? This can only be described as the height of white supremacist arrogance.

The power of the entertainment industry to rewrite history has been used to rewrite wars from the Vietnam war to the world wars to the wars in the Middle East. The narrative is always that the West is engaged in a battle between good and evil and for good to prevail, wars have to be fought. We live in a world that is so full of lies, so full of narrative management, so full of brainwashing and manipulation that it is no exaggeration to say that everything we know about every war that has ever been fought is a lie. It follows therefore that everything we are being told today about the wars that are being fought is a lie. The narratives we are given to convince us that war is a necessity are made up because there is no reason countries cannot get along with each other, just the same way people get along with their neighbours without resorting to physical violence whenever they disagree. If human beings were as aggressive as we are made to believe, then we would never be able to get along with our neighbours or our colleagues at work. Why then is it that countries supposedly cannot get along without war? This is a blatant lie fed to us by the very elites who benefit from these wars.

Reinforcing the illusions of war

The reason people agree to go to war is that they have been brainwashed into believing certain illusions. One of these illusions is the idea that wars have winners and losers. For example, we are told that the allies won the second world war. But if we look at the facts on the ground, we realize that most of the countries that were involved in the war were left damaged beyond recognition. Millions of lives were lost on all sides of the war. Economies were destroyed. Buildings and infrastructure were destroyed. How is it that people whose countries were devastated by war ended up believing that they somehow won? The reality is that no one wins in a war. The idea that one side wins is a lie created by those who benefit from war. These people have no qualms about risking other people's lives - young men and women who would otherwise have lived long and productive lives - in pursuit of their illusions. We see this lie propagated time and again in the entertainment media. Movies that deal with war are always portrayed in terms of winners and losers, with one side portrayed as the winner and the other side portrayed as the loser. This is brainwashing. We are told that the atomic bombs that were dropped at Hiroshima and Nagasaki ended World War II and led to the allies winning the war. This is pure propaganda. The dropping of these atomic bombs was an evil act whose consequences continued for decades. How anyone could frame this as a positive event is beyond comprehension. Only severe brainwashing could make us believe the lies we are continually fed by the elites about their wars.

Another illusion that is reinforced by the entertainment industry is the idea that going to war is a heroic act that should be applauded by all. Soldiers are heroes who "give their lives" so that the rest of us can enjoy our freedoms. The reality is that these soldiers do not "give their lives" but rather have their lives snatched away from them by a ruthless war machine. We have been brainwashed into overriding our natural drive to preserve life. We have been manipulated into thinking that it is heroic to put ourselves in situations that shorten our lifespans. We have been brainwashed into thinking that people who do not want to go to war are cowards. Since when did it become heroic to want to shorten one's life? Yet we have allowed the elites to manipulate us into believing this. Why is it that war has been made into an exception in which all the normal rules we live by are set aside? Just because we call an activity "war", suddenly it becomes okay to kill, maim, destroy and steal. It is time we saw through this lie. The entertainment industry as usual plays its role in getting us to accept this brainwashing. Almost every movie we watch dealing with war makes it appear heroic to want to go to war. It is almost as if we put aside our normal thinking brains and enter into a state of hypnosis in which outlandish ideas suddenly become acceptable.

Another illusion that is reinforced by the entertainment industry is the idea that there are righteous wars. The logic behind this is that the end justifies the means. According to this logic, in order to achieve some righteous goal, it is sometimes necessary to do evil. This evil is somehow supposed to result in good. This is an illogical idea. Evil only leads to more evil, because it traps one in an action-reaction spiral that eventually becomes self-reinforcing. If you commit an evil act, it makes it easier for you to commit another evil act and if you continue long enough in this cycle, you reach a point where it becomes inevitable that one evil act will lead to another. It becomes almost impossible to disentangle oneself from the downward spiral. Therefore, the idea that an evil act could result in good is a lie. This is the reason wars are so unpredictable. You start a war thinking it will end quickly and painlessly with a positive result, but something unexpected happens that changes the equation and takes you deeper into the quagmire. The enemy reacts in ways no one anticipated, they turn out to be stronger than expected or they happen to get support from somewhere you would never have imagined. In this way, what was meant to be a quick "shock and awe" bogs down a country for decades in needless bloodshed and destruction. Anyone going into war thinking it will have a predictable outcome is deluding themselves. Hollywood is good at reinforcing this particular illusion. We are shown the heroic West going into war as a matter of principle against an evil enemy on the other side. The West is portrayed as the defender of humanity that has a right to intervene everywhere on the planet to ensure the world remains safe for all. In reality, these interventions keep the world in a constant state of war that is not going to end until we let go of these illusions.

Glorifying violence

The entertainment industry has consistently fed humanity a steady diet of violence that is gradually getting worse. It is rare to watch anything these days that doesn't include some form of violence. Violence has been made to appear normal and the natural response to any provocation. Human beings are portrayed as violent by nature and worse still, this is made to look like a good thing. Think of all the action movies we watch today in which the protagonist is a violent, lawless type who doesn't care about anything other than winning. Anyone who stands in their way is destroyed because whatever end they are pursuing is worth any amount of carnage. The nature of the violence on our screens also seems to be getting worse every day. It is no longer enough to show a person being killed; nowadays the death has to be as gruesome, bloody and gory as possible.   It is almost as if there is a deliberate attempt not just to shock, but to reduce if not eliminate our sensitivity and aversion to violence.   It makes one wonder why Hollywood in particular seems to be so invested in desensitizing us to violence. Is it maybe because they are part of the same elites who work together to push humanity towards more violence and wars? Is the entertainment industry knowingly brainwashing humanity to view violence as a normal and acceptable part of life? I believe they are. I believe they are part of the same global elites who work together with the end goal of global domination.

Human beings naturally have an instinct to preserve life. No one wants to die before their time. How then do the elites get people who would otherwise be fully invested in living long, productive lives to willingly enlist in the war machine and sacrifice their lives for causes that have nothing to do with them? How do the elites override the instinct to preserve life? By brainwashing us into believing that violence is the natural response to any slight. We are brainwashed into believing that when provoked, violence is the right response. We are brainwashed into believing that when a neighbouring country does something we do not agree with, then the natural response is to want to destroy them. How do you teach people to respond in this unnatural way? By bombarding them with "entertainment" that teaches them a certain way of being. By teaching them to bypass all other methods of conflict resolution and painting the world as a place in which violence is the only way people resolve conflict.

Many of us are impacted by the violence on our screens without us even knowing it. We may think that we abhor violence, but internally we have been brainwashed into believing that violence is sometimes inevitable. We have been brainwashed into thinking that even though no one wants violence, sometimes there are no other options. For example, if someone hurts our loved one, then it becomes acceptable to react with violence even though we are not normally violent by nature. If our country is threatened, it becomes necessary to put aside our aversion to violence and do whatever the government tells us to do. This is how the elites manage to bypass our moral compasses, by brainwashing us into believing that there are always exceptions. Many of us walk around believing ourselves to be averse to violence, but we may not be aware that deep inside our subconscious minds lay certain beliefs that would cause us to bypass our natural aversion to violence. These beliefs are the ones the elites tap into when they need to get people to take up arms against an enemy. All they have to do is make us feel afraid and threatened by the enemy and we immediately set aside our life-preserving instincts. Even we can be surprised by the violence of our reactions. If you have ever wondered why the Nazis convinced the German people to commit genocide or why the Rwandans committed genocide against their people, it is because of these beliefs that lie in our subconscious minds. These beliefs that are constantly being reinforced tell us that in certain circumstances, it is okay to set aside our morality in order to survive or defend ourselves. These beliefs lie out of reach of our conscious minds waiting for the right trigger to activate them. That is why the elites must constantly reinforce these latent beliefs through the entertainment we watch, among other things. We need to understand that brainwashing people *en masse* is not something that just happens by chance. It takes a very concerted effort to brainwash people and override their instincts. This is why the entertainment industry bombards us with scenes of violence. You could be watching a romance or a comedy when suddenly out of nowhere, you encounter a violent scene. When this happens repeatedly, we become desensitized to the violence. We start seeing it as normal. We stop being horrified by it. We start seeing it as a normal way for people to react. We start expecting people to react with violence when provoked. These attitudes seep into our subconscious minds, ready to be activated by the elites when they call upon us to go to war.

To overcome this very aggressive push by the entertainment industry, we need to be aware of what they are doing and actively resist it. We need to be aware that this glorification of violence is not just accidental - it is intended to change the way we think. It is targeted at our subconscious minds where beliefs and attitudes can be implanted and used against us. Once we have this awareness, we can approach the entertainment industry with a new awareness and thus stop the process of being brainwashed against our will. Awareness is the first step. Knowing that there is a malicious intent to this is the first step towards freeing ourselves.

Keeping people distracted

Life is hard. For many if not most people on earth, life is nothing more than a constant struggle for survival. We run around from morning to evening working in jobs we don't like, interacting with people we don't like and doing boring, repetitive tasks. If we had an option, most of us would much rather be somewhere else doing something else. Our employers push us to produce more and dedicate ourselves wholly to our jobs. As soon as you arrive at the workplace, you are expected to push aside your individuality and become a mechanized robot whose only role is to produce. Under the guise of professionalism, we are forced to operate like machines that have no opinions, no feelings, no ideas and no need to be happy or fulfilled. We are forced to operate as if all we want in life is to earn money. We are not allowed to appear as if we have lives outside of our workplace. We are not expected to allow our "personal lives" to interfere with our professional lives. In other words, working means putting aside our humanity. Since we are human beings with emotions, feelings and desires, this takes a toll on us. We become stressed, unhappy and unfulfilled. Life becomes meaningless. We are forced to suppress that part of us that wants to experience life in its fulness. We are forced to accept less than what we desire and to bury that part of us that is curious, creative and joyous. We become nothing more than biological robots whose only function is survival.

This is the state into which man has sunk. Not only have we been turned into biological robots, but we don't seem to realize that this has happened. We take for granted that the way we live life is the only way life can be lived. We do what we have been programmed to do, which is to live lives that are solely dedicated to survival. It never occurs to us that there could be more to life than mere survival. We long ago forgot that we are spiritual beings that are here to experience life in all its glorious potential. We dare not peek behind the curtain to see what lies beyond the prison walls because it is too risky. Our very lives depend on us living within the matrix that has been constructed for us. We no longer see the prison walls because the programming is so successful that it never even occurs to us that we are in prison. We have been taught to admire the elites from afar while deceiving ourselves that if we only worked hard enough, pushed ourselves hard enough and denied ourselves enough, we would eventually become like them. The truth of course is that the more we push ourselves, the more money we make for them.

This is where the entertainment industry comes in. How do you get people to become biological robots who do your bidding without them realizing that this is what is happening? You keep them distracted. You keep them busy with meaningless entertainment that makes them forget how miserable they are. You keep them emersed in fantasy worlds that have nothing to do with their real lives. You blunt their feelings of hopelessness and helplessness by giving them the illusion, at least for a few hours that they could be like the celebrities they watch on television. You give them the impression that whatever they are watching is attainable while simultaneously making them feel that there is something wrong with them for not attaining it. You give them the feeling that they are to blame for their miserable lives. But most of all, you keep them so focused on meaningless entertainment that they will never remember to look inside themselves because if they did, they would remember that they are spiritual beings, extensions of the creator, made in his image and here to seek oneness with him.

If people stopped running for a moment and slowed down a bit, they would start thinking about the bigger questions of life. They would start asking themselves who they are and what they are doing here. They would start wondering how they got to be on this planet and what they are supposed to be doing. These kinds of questions cannot be asked by people who are too busy chasing money and too tired to do anything afterwards, other than sit in front of their television sets and lose themselves in a make-believe world. People who are tired, stressed and unfulfilled cannot look beyond the daily struggle for survival. Conversely, people who are content, fulfilled and happy will eventually start longing for oneness with their creator. Because as spiritual beings, we are not here to just engage in a mindless pursuit of money or mere survival. We are here to have experiences that take us closer to oneness with our source. The elites obviously cannot understand this because they long ago sold their souls to the god of money and power. They cannot understand their spiritual origin and to them, this kind of talk is stupidity. No wonder the first thing they do in totalitarianism is to abolish religion or make themselves gods. They will do anything to prevent people from waking up to the reality of who they are as spiritual beings because this threatens the carefully constructed illusion that they are superior beings who have the right to rule over everyone else.

If we were not so distracted, we would be able to look at our world and start questioning many of the assumptions we have. Why is the world the way it is? Is the mess we are in an inevitable part of life on this planet or is there anything we can do to change it? Why do we continue having wars on this planet? Why do we keep allowing the elites to manipulate us into going to war against our brothers and sisters in other parts of the world? Why do we listen to politicians when they tell us that we need to sacrifice ourselves, our beloved children, our lives and our livelihoods to fight wars? Why do we believe our leaders when they tell us that others are a threat, enemies that we should be willing to destroy? If we were not so distracted, we would question what our leaders tell us. We would question the necessity for wars. We would ask ourselves why diplomacy cannot work to resolve whatever differences we have with our neighbours. We would start noticing that these differences are caused by the very leaders who claim to have the solution to the problem. This is what the entertainment industry does. It keeps us distracted from the bigger questions of life and keeps our attention focused on non-issues while the "big boys" run the world. These big boys unfortunately are not capable of running the world. Their greed and thirst for power will always keep causing chaos for the rest of us. The average person on the streets would probably make a much better leader than many of the people who today call themselves world leaders. If you have empathy and love for your brothers and sisters, you are already much more qualified than they will ever be. It is time we stopped allowing ourselves to be manipulated and reclaimed our right to live in a peaceful world.

Chapter 5
Questioning your Worldview

Whenever war breaks out in any part of the world, any observant person will immediately notice a certain pattern begin to unfold. The first thing that happens is that the mainstream media aggressively comes in with a narrative about what is happening. The media quickly gives us their interpretation of what is happening, for example painting one side as the aggressor while the other side is painted as the victim. Next, we are informed of attempts at diplomacy, but we are never allowed to have much faith in this diplomacy which is made to appear doomed from the beginning. Then, we hear of debates taking place at the United Nations, with this country claiming one thing and that country claiming another, but eventually, we stop hearing about the debates altogether and we never get to know what the conclusion was. Finally, the media narrative becomes monopolised by "experts" whose powerful voices - invariably pro-war - share their opinions on how the war is going and who is likely to win. Gradually, people lose interest in the war and move on with their lives. They assume that whatever they hear in the media is the gospel truth and never think to question the narrative. People come to believe that matters of war are best left to the experts, i.e., the politicians, the generals, the think tanks and former military officials who are in a better position to understand what is happening. We come to rely on these people to tell us how to think about war and we stop trusting ourselves to have valid opinions. Any opinion we might have about war appears naïve or uninformed. The fact that there is a special lingua that is applied when discussing war further makes us feel like we have no business discussing war or having an opinion about it. The interesting thing is that sometimes the things we are told by the "experts" are so illogical, it should immediately be obvious that we are being lied to. But because we have spent all our lives being sold a certain worldview, we somehow believe the unbelievable. For example, during the Russia-Ukraine war, we were told that the West stood for peace in Ukraine even while they sent tonnes of weapons to Ukraine. If you apply logic to this idea, it immediately becomes nonsensical. Why would the West flood Ukraine with weapons if they wanted peace? Wouldn't it make more sense to support diplomatic efforts to help bring the war to an end? Isn't it logical that sending more weapons only worsens and prolongs the war while turning Ukraine into a war zone for years to come? But somehow, the media spins this as a good thing and a helpful gesture on the part of the West. This kind of illogical reasoning should make us start questioning everything we have ever been told about war.

Who shapes our worldview on war?

Human beings have very specific ideas about what the world is supposed to look like. Some of these ideas are so ingrained that we never even stop to question them. Our political systems. Our geopolitical systems. Our education systems. Our social lives. The way we work. The way we love. We accept that the world is the way it is because that is the way it is supposed to be. But have you ever asked yourself where we get our ideas about what the world is supposed to look like? Are the systems we have the only possible systems we could have on the planet? The truth of the matter is that the way the world works today is the result of ideas that come from human beings. There is nothing to say that these systems are necessarily the best systems or the only possible systems. Neither can we say that these systems come from God because they seem to contradict everything we know about God's nature. Our world is based on a competitive model in which the winner takes all. This is not the only way that our world could be structured. We could have a world that is based on cooperation, whereby we see ourselves as being in the same boat, therefore needing to cooperate in order 3efto survive and thrive. Unfortunately, we have been brainwashed into believing that being competitive is the only way human beings can exist. From the day we are born, our parents pass on these attitudes to us. They do their best to prepare us to exist in a competitive world by doing whatever they can to give us a head start. In this way, they are already telling us that we will need to fight to survive. When we go to school, it is the same thing. Our education system is structured in a way that teaches us to always compete with each other. We are taught to see our fellow students as competition that we need to beat. We are taught to see ourselves in comparison with others. not as human beings in our own right. We are taught that we are not good enough unless we are ahead of others. We are taught that our worth comes from scoring the highest grades and being at the top of the class. If, God forbid, we do not perform well, then we are taught that we have less value than those who are at the top. This same attitude extends to the workplace where we are taught that to get ahead, we have to be better than everyone else. We have to work harder than anyone, produce the best results and do anything to please our bosses. If need be, we should be willing to step on others or ride on their backs to get ahead. Outside of the workplace, we are taught to compete with others in society; to buy the latest cars, live in the best houses and wear the most fashionable clothes. This is done not to live our best lives but to keep up with or outdo our neighbours. We want our marriages to be picture-perfect and our children to attend the best schools, all so that we feel that we are better than others.

I hope you can see where I'm going with this. We have been brainwashed into believing that life is a competition against others. Instead of living life in ways that make us happy, we drive ourselves almost to death in order to be better than others. We live life in comparison with others and in the process, we lose ourselves. Where does this idea about life come from? What happened is that over time, we allowed the most aggressive people amongst us to be the ones deciding how the world should be structured. These people see life only as a competition and they somehow managed to get the rest of us to look at life this way. They deceived us into looking at life the same way they look at it and into structuring the world in a competitive rather than cooperative way. The most aggressive people captured our collective psyches and instilled in us the idea that human beings are supposed to compete with each other over scarce resources. The very idea that the world has scarce resources comes from these same aggressive beings. Every day we are told that the world is running out of resources to support human beings. The truth, however, is that we have a *distribution* problem, whereby the world's wealth and resources are hoarded by a few, meaning that the rest have to do without. If these resources could be distributed equitably, we would not have people going hungry or living in poverty in certain parts of the world. The idea that the world has limited resources is a false narrative created by the most aggressive among us who would prefer that no one questioned the fact that they have amongst themselves almost 90% of the world's wealth. These are the same people who meet every year at Davos for the World Economic Forum (WEF) and pretend to come up with solutions for the world's problems. This is akin to a meeting of wolves trying to solve the problem of sheep being eaten at night.   Or as someone once said, it is like attending a firefighter's conference where no one is allowed to talk about water. It is no surprise therefore that the kind of solutions these people come up with include dystopian scenarios in which we own nothing, have no privacy and are happy about it. This is simply an expression of their disdain for humanity, that they could come up with such ideas and seriously put them forth as solutions to the world's problems.

When it comes to war, our worldview is equally shaped by aggressive people holding leadership positions in policy-making institutions. How else do you explain the fact that even though most people do not want to go to war and are innately anti-war, we continue having wars on the planet? How do you explain the fact that even though most of humanity is horrified by the idea of nuclear war, we seem to be marching closer and closer to a nuclear confrontation between nuclear-armed nations? The people driving the agenda are lost in a delusional worldview in which having the most powerful and destructive weapons equals being the most powerful nation on earth. These lunatics who have zero ability to reason intelligently are the ones driving the agenda and they keep taking us closer and closer to annihilation. It is no exaggeration to say that the people leading our world are mentally ill in the literal sense of the word. They are psychopaths and narcissists who should be locked up in mental health institutions or at the very least under psychiatric care, not the ones making the most important decisions on earth. How humanity allowed such a situation to exist is something we will have to grapple with for a long time as we start waking up to the reality of our situation.

The ideas we hold about war come from the war industry which is run by the most aggressive, war-like people on earth. The same primitive ideas our forefathers held about fighting for land and resources are still held by these people today, at a time when we should long ago have transcended such ideas. The days of fighting others for land and resources should by now be part of our forgotten history, together with things like making fire from sticks. In our modern world, no one should be thinking about stealing land and resources, and in all fairness, most people on earth don't think like this. But those who run the global agenda still do. They are like toddlers in adult bodies, fighting each other over toys. We can therefore conclude that the ones running the world have the lowest consciousness among humanity. These people are driven by greed for power and profits, the same way wild animals are driven by the urge to kill prey for food. Instead of using their God-given intelligence to temper this desire with reason, they foolishly follow their lower instincts and drag the rest of humanity along with them. They spread their ideologies through think tanks that push their aggressive ideas on the rest of the world. They lobby politicians to pass laws and policies that favour their war-mongering. They buy up the mainstream media and use it as a conduit for their narratives. And they brainwash us through the entertainment industry that glorifies war and violence. This, in a nutshell, is how they infect the entire human race with their primitive worldview.

Is war normal?

Imagine your neighbour did something that made you angry or upset. Would you take a gun and shoot them? Would you burn down their house? Would you kill their family? For most of us, it is obvious that we wouldn't do this. If we did, we would immediately be arrested and sent to prison. We would not be allowed to remain in society but would be sent away to keep us from the rest of society. The reason of course is that this is abnormal behaviour, behaviour that is unacceptable in any civilised society. We all know and agree that we cannot survive if we allow violence in society. We do everything in our power to eliminate violence from society and invest considerably to keep violent people at bay. Anyone who commits violence against other members of society is relentlessly hunted down and brought to justice. We do not allow the idea to take hold that someone can be violent and get away with it. Whether it is domestic violence or any other form of violence, we refuse to co-exist with violence because we understand that it endangers all of us. Yet for some reason, we continue to accept the idea that one country should be able to attack and unleash violence on another country. We invest considerable resources towards building armies and buying weapons that could one day be used against another country. Why this cognitive dissonance? Why do we abhor violence within our society but find it acceptable that one country should unleash violence upon other people in distant lands? Why are we not able to see that people that are far away from us are no different from us, no less deserving of peaceful existence on this planet? If we cannot even bear the thought of our children being attacked and killed by an invading army, why would we allow our country to do the same to another country? Don't we see that all human beings on this planet have an equal right to exist peacefully without violence? Why is it obvious to us that we cannot co-exist with violence in our societies yet hold on to the idea that it is okay to be violent towards neighbouring countries? How did we end up believing this lie and becoming so comfortable with it?

The first mistake we made is to believe that human beings are not created equal. Once the violent, aggressive people in our midst got us to believe this, then from there more lies could be built upon that one lie. If human beings had resisted this original lie, we would not have the evils we have on this planet such as war, slavery or colonialism. We first had to believe that some people are inferior to others and from there it became acceptable to reason that it is okay to kill, enslave and oppress them. Once we believed that some people are less than others, it became possible to reason that the inferior people should serve the superior ones. Until we overcome this original lie, we will never be able to overcome the evils on this planet. That is why war is normalized on this planet. People are not able to see the humanity in other people and therefore it does not disturb them to think about people having to flee their homes with bullets and bombs raining down upon them. If we could see other people's humanity, we would never allow our governments to attack them and cause them so much suffering. The people in the West who consider themselves the most civilized people on earth do not bat an eye at the idea that their governments are killing women and children in other parts of the world. They do not see other people as deserving of the very freedoms their governments pretend to be defending on their behalf.

To heal our planet, we need to reject the idea that people are not created equal. We are all human beings wanting the same things in life whether we are black, brown or white and whether we live in Africa, Asia, Europe or the Americas. We are all the same. There is no one better than the other. Once we see through this lie, we will not be willing to accept that anyone in any part of the world should be killed by another and we will start demanding that our governments immediately stop this evil. War is not normal. It is time we rejected the normalization of war and demanded peace for everyone on the planet. The idea that any part of the world should be at war is unacceptable.

Are human beings inherently violent?

Historians tell us that human beings were not always at war with each other. At some point in our history, we started killing each other and that has continued to this day. The question is, what happened to cause us to start killing each other and how do we stop? One theory is that humanity is made up of a small percentage of people suffering from Anti-Social Personality Disorder (ASPD), the people commonly known as psychopaths or sociopaths. According to this theory, when conditions are right, these people who number about 1-4% of the population start coming together and forming groups or gangs which then start causing trouble within the community. One of the conditions that need to be met is that the population must be large enough to allow enough of the ASPD sufferers to meet each other and interact with each other. When the general population is too low, the chances of these people coming together to cause trouble are low as they are dispersed within the population. The problem comes once the population becomes large because the number of such people also increases and the probability that they will meet and band together to cause trouble increases. This is when you start having gangs within the community and in extreme situations, these gangs organise themselves into organised crime syndicates such as the mafia and they take over a community. When these people succeed in manipulating themselves into positions of power, that is when the real trouble begins. There is a big difference between Hitler when he was an obscure troublemaker causing riots in the streets and when he managed to manipulate his way into a position of power in Germany. When he managed to get into a position of power, that is when he was able to get people to commit the atrocities we read about today. The theory of the trouble-making psychopaths perfectly fills the gap in our understanding as to why historically human beings did not have war and why gradually, we started the war-like activities we see today. The missing link is that as the human population grew, so too did the influence of the people with ASPD who could now come into contact with each other and have an outlet for their aggressive tendencies. Once they started meeting and reinforcing each other's criminality, they were able to organise and overwhelm the communities in which they existed. From there it was only a matter of time before they manipulated or forced their way into leadership positions, allowing them to cause untold suffering to their societies. The irony is that most of the people we revere as heroes of past ages are criminally insane individuals who were able to capture whole societies and cause them to go to war with others.

Unfortunately, today many people have come to believe that human beings are all inherently violent, which is why there is never any serious attempt to eliminate war on the planet. We have allowed ourselves to be deceived and manipulated into violent and aggressive behaviours that go against our very nature. As long as we continue allowing psychopaths to gain leadership positions, we will continue having wars on this planet. These people will never stop their war-like tendencies because they are violent by nature. It is time humanity woke up and decided that we no longer want to be led by mentally ill people. We need to get to a point where people aspiring for leadership positions, whether CEOs or politicians get screened for ASPD. We know today that psychopaths are very well represented among the top leadership positions in business and politics. What we may not yet have accepted is just how much damage these people do to society and the planet as a whole. Once we start accepting this, then we can start treating this issue with the seriousness it deserves and even demanding that leaders undergo psychological tests as a basic requirement for holding leadership positions. In this way, we will eliminate psychopathy in leadership and we will start living in a world in which peace is valued and actively sought. As long as mentally ill, aggressive people are running the world and setting the agenda, we will never have peace. To them, peace is for cowards while aggression and competition indicate strength. We need to reject this worldview and reject the insane people behind this worldview.

Is war sometimes justified?

While most people on earth detest war, we have unfortunately been brainwashed into thinking that it is sometimes justified. We have been led to believe that sometimes the provocations are so egregious that we cannot let them go. A good example is the September 11 bombing in the United States which was supposedly such a gross violation of America's sovereignty that it had to be responded to with war. More recently, we had the provocations against Russia by NATO in which Russia supposedly had no choice but to respond militarily by attacking Ukraine. Other examples abound both historically and more recently. There appears to be a very peculiar belief among human beings that sometimes, normal beliefs and morality have to be set aside in order to respond to certain wrongs. At such times, talk of peace is seen as cowardly and unpatriotic by those who believe that war is the only appropriate response. But the question is, who wants a war in which their loved ones are killed or forced to flee their homes? What could be more natural than the desire for peace?

The idea that war is sometimes justified is a lie that has been cleverly weaved into our collective consciousness by the people who benefit from war. The uncritical, non-stop coverage of wars by the mainstream media is not accidental. They constantly push their aggressive narratives onto the rest of the world giving the impression that there is no other way to think about war. They use nonsensical arguments that would be laughable were it not for the fact that their consequences are so severe. War against terror? War against drugs? War to protect freedom and democracy? Righteous strikes? How do we buy such arguments? The truth is that war is NEVER justified. There is never any justification for attacking people, killing them, forcing them out of their homes and destroying their property. The only people who would think it justified to behave this way are psychopaths who do not value life and who have no guilt or conscience. Normal, sane people would sit down and come up with solutions to their disagreements. They would use mediation if they cannot agree. They would go to court if mediation does not work. This is how civilized society works. The only reason diplomacy fails and talks collapse is that the psychopaths in these talks will never accept compromise even if it means millions of deaths. Normal people would naturally be willing to compromise if the alternative is the deaths of many people. The sooner we wake up to the fact that we are being manipulated by people who do not value human life and who keep leading us towards war, the sooner we will reject their worldview and start having peace on this planet.

Is war sometimes inevitable?

There are certain scenarios in which we are led to believe that war is inevitable. In other words, despite everyone's goodwill and best intentions, war simply cannot be avoided. An example of this is the war in the Middle East between Palestine and Israel. Despite decades of attempts at peace, there appears to be no end in sight. The unending spiral of violence seems to be a problem that can never be solved. My take on this is that there are hidden forces that will not allow a peaceful resolution no matter what anyone does. I don't see how peace talks can last for decades without coming up with meaningful results. The only conclusion is that the peace talks are not being held in good faith. I believe there are people within the process who will not allow a peaceful resolution because it benefits them to keep the war going. These people will keep blocking any reasonable concessions and will continue taking a hard-line stance that keeps the process from moving forward. How exactly they benefit from this is anyone's guess; it could be from the weapon sales or the continuation of the "special" relationship with the United States. Something does not add up in this generations-old conflict.

Just think of how ridiculous it is for people to spend generations fighting over a small piece of land. Is it truly impossible to arrive at some logical conclusion that everyone can live with? What could be so special about this piece of land that could cause people to spend generations fighting over it? This situation reminds me of a situation a few years ago in Kenya when a small island between Kenya and Uganda became the subject of controversy. The Ugandan military had supposedly started chasing Kenyan fishermen from the island on which the two neighbours had co-existed peacefully for a long time.

When the story hit the news, many people took on a war-like stance insisting that Kenya needed to go to war with Uganda to protest the injustice. Some people even took matters into their own hands by damaging part of the railway line that passed through Kenya to Uganda as a way to sabotage Uganda's economy. Fortunately, we had a wise leader, President Mwai Kibaki who did not allow himself to be drawn into an emotional reaction. Eventually, the controversy died down. Imagine if he had taken a hard-line stance and Kenya had gone to war with Uganda over a tiny piece of land. What a foolish, needless course of action. The point of this is that two groups of people fighting each other over some disputed piece of land for generations just seems unreasonable. All it would take for peace to prevail would be for one side to remain calm in the face of provocation. Justice could be pursued at the United Nations or through international legal mechanisms such as the International Court of Justice. Kenya currently has a case at this very court with our neighbour Somalia over some disputed territory in the Indian Ocean. How much better to handle such matters in a civilised manner than to resort to war? If there was good faith in the Palestine / Israel issue, this conflict would have been resolved a long time ago. The reality is that no war is unavoidable. No problem does not have a solution. With our normal, God-given capacity for negotiation and conflict resolution, there is no way that decades and generations of talks could take place with no solution like the apparently "unsolvable" conflict in the Middle East.

Does war have winners and losers?

Yet another lie we have been programmed to believe is that wars have winners and losers. War is portrayed as a competition in which one side could win while the other side loses. We see this clearly in the Russia-Ukraine war in which the Western media keeps pushing the idea that Ukraine is winning while the Russian media insists that Russia is winning. Both of these positions are nothing more than propaganda. If you take a moment to think about what "winning" means in the context of war, you will realize that it is a completely false narrative. How do you win a war? By killing more people than the enemy? By driving people from their homes and taking their property? By destroying towns and cities? How could this possibly be termed as winning? When soldiers go back home having lost their colleagues, suffering from PTSD, having sustained physical injuries or been maimed for life and being driven to suicide, how could anyone term this a win? Can you imagine how much programming has gone into getting humanity to believe such a preposterous idea? When you look at it this way, the idea that war has winners and losers loses all meaning. When people go into a mindset in which they want to destroy others and do everything in their power to achieve this, I think it is fair to say that there can be no winners or losers. We talk of winners and losers when referring to a competition in which there are clear rules for winning and losing. We can talk of winners and losers in a race whereby the first person to arrive is the winner. In this case, the rules of the competition are clear and even a neutral observer can see that one person won and the other one lost. Can we refer to war as a competition? What are the criteria for winning? What yardstick to we use to measure who has won and who has lost?

I hope you are starting to see what I mean when I say that the idea that war has winners and losers is meaningless. Competition as applied to war is meaningless. It is a false narrative that we have been programmed to believe and this is what keeps wars going. When soldiers come out of a war with the idea that they won or the world tells them that they won, this motivates them and others to engage in more senseless wars. This propaganda keeps the world blinded by the delusional idea that war is a competition with winners and losers. Rather than focusing on the damage and wanton destruction caused by war and realising that there can never be winners and losers in such chaos, we have accepted the false idea that one side can emerge as the winner. This is nothing but propaganda. The side with the loudest and most effective propaganda machine will simply declare itself the winner and write history to reflect this. History is full of false narratives of one side winning and the other side losing. A closer study of the reality will show that war is nothing but a chaotic activity in which people set aside their humanity in order to engage in the senseless destruction of lives and property for the benefit of the people hiding behind the scenes. It is not a competition. There are no winners and losers.

This false notion that wars have winners and losers causes us to honour the worst murderers in history by calling them heroes. Today, people are starting to wake up to just how much deception has gone into what we call history, which is often just a creation of delusional minds. People in many parts of the world are starting to demand the taking down of monuments honouring these war criminals. Unfortunately, many among us still prefer to hold on to the consciousness of war and these are the people who violently oppose the bringing down of these monuments. We are seeing a gradual awakening among people in the West that colonialism was not merely empire-building but the brutal subjugation of people deemed to be inferior. It is important for such an awakening to take place otherwise we are doomed to repeat history. That false idea held by some Westerners that empire was something to be proud of is something that must start giving way to a true understanding of what colonialism was. Just like slavery or apartheid, it was nothing to be proud of. If the world is to start moving away from war as a fact of life in the 21st century, we need to start looking at our history honestly and transcend the consciousness that caused us to behave so callously towards our fellow man.

Do the ends justify the means?

The idea that the ends justify the means has been used to justify a lot of evil on this planet. This idea has been so ingrained in us that we believe it is sometimes justified to ignore God's commands in order to achieve some righteous purpose. Historically, this idea was used to justify the brutal oppression of humanity by the catholic church whereby millions were killed for "heresy", meaning that they dared to believe something contrary to what the catholic church defined as the truth. The catholic church deemed it appropriate to torture and murder human beings in the name of God. Somehow, they managed to sell the idea that defending the truth was worth any human cost. This same idea is reinforced today through the movies we watch in which one person destroys lives and property in pursuit of some obscure goal and this is deemed heroic. What we are being programmed to believe is that sometimes there can be a goal so important, so righteous that it is okay to set aside our humanity, our morality and our beliefs to achieve this goal. Most of us unfortunately have been deceived by this mentality, which is why we are willing to look away when our governments invade other countries. We are taught to believe that in the interest of protecting our freedoms and democracy, we sometimes have to be cruel, have to use force or have to use violence.

If the world is to transcend war, one of the beliefs we need to get rid of is the belief that the ends justify the means. As long as human beings hold on to this lie, we will continue committing cruel acts against our brothers and sisters in the name of some worthwhile goal. We have been manipulated into taking on ideas that come from the most ruthless people amongst us who see nothing wrong with murder. Instead of aspiring to higher ideals, we continue taking on the ideas of the lowest among us. We have examples we can emulate such as Nelson Mandela, who despite his cruel treatment at the hands of the apartheid regime taught us how to treat those who mistreat us. This is what caused South Africa to peacefully come out of apartheid. Black South Africans could have decided to take revenge for the suffering they endured, but instead, they followed the example of forgiveness set by Mandela. Who said peaceful resistance cannot achieve results? We also saw an example of non-violent resistance in Mahatma Gandhi who successfully led India out of British colonial rule. Why can't we follow the example of the people among us with the highest consciousness rather than follow those with the lowest ideas?

To overcome the consciousness that the ends justify the means, we have to start by examining ourselves to see if we carry this belief in our subconscious minds. What do we believe at the core of our being about war? When we hear that war has broken out in some part of the world, how does that make us feel? Do we believe the narratives that we see in the mainstream media? Do we doubt the media narrative or do we accept without question that that's just the way the world works? Do we ever question our worldview about the necessity of war? Do we ever question what our leaders tell us about the need to go to war? Do we find ourselves setting aside our beliefs and morality when we are told that there is a good reason for it? Do we believe that God intended the commandment "thou shalt not murder" to apply 100% of the time or do we believe that sometimes we have to set it aside? To discover if you have been affected by the idea that the ends justify the means, ask yourself what you feel about the wars that are taking place on the planet right now. If you can think of at least one war that you feel is justified for one reason or the other, then you are a victim of the belief that the ends justify the means. If you believe that it is not possible to eliminate war because sometimes, we have no choice but to react with violence or to set aside the laws of God, then you need to question your worldview. If you live in the United States and firmly believe that it is justified for people to have guns for self-defence, then you have taken on the belief that the ends justify the means. This belief system will only result in an increasing spiral of violence. Until we understand that God's laws apply 100% of the time, then we have no hope of eliminating war on this planet.

The lie of the peacekeeping force

The "peacekeeping force" is a very interesting concept that has been developed by the West. According to this concept, you can stop a war by sending soldiers to fight the people that are fighting in the war. If that sounds confusing, that's because it is. How can you stop a war by sending more soldiers to the battlefield? This line of reasoning has been used by everyone from the United Nations to countries that want to intervene in a conflict. We are somehow supposed to believe that the people intervening in wars are benevolent beings with no other motive other than to help the people end the fighting. We are supposed to believe that there are "good" forces that want to stop the war and there are forces of evil that must be stopped at any cost. This lie is something we need to see through and reject. It has become such a common myth that Russia used it when it invaded Ukraine. The question is, how come we could easily see through Russia's false claims whereas we have trouble seeing through the West's many false claims of sending peacekeeping forces to stop wars? It is probably because we have been programmed for a long time to see the West as good and benevolent and everyone else as evil. We are programmed to see the West's actions as righteous and necessary no matter how despicable they are. The West has been so successful in its campaign to come across as big brother, defending freedom and democracy on the planet that we never even stop to question their claims or motivations. Whenever they intervene in any part of the world be it Libya, Syria, Iraq or Afghanistan, we are always assured that their motives are pure.

We saw this very lie used in West Africa, with France meddling in African affairs under the guise of helping stop terrorists. Sending more arms and soldiers into a war is no different from pouring fuel into a fire. It doesn't take a genius to see that the reason France sent forces to West Africa was to gain influence in the region. Unlike other colonial powers who long ago left their former colonies, France still insists on maintaining a stranglehold on her former colonies. It is almost as if they fear that letting go of West Africa will make them irrelevant on the world stage. Therefore, the peacekeeping force is nothing but an excuse to maintain a presence in the region. It is no exaggeration to say that every time we hear of a peacekeeping force being sent somewhere, there is usually a hidden agenda at play. Fortunately, West Africa is waking up and demanding that France leaves the region. The question is whether France is willing to accept the sovereignty of West African people and leave quietly or whether they will use underhand means to remain in the region. Only time will tell.

I related in a previous chapter how Kenya almost sank into civil war following a disputed election. How did the country manage to pull itself out of this? It was through the efforts of a group of eminent African leaders led by Kofi Annan, who worked tirelessly for months to bring the various parties to the table for peace talks. In the end, after months of talks, they managed to bring the parties together in a handshake that saw an end to the violence. To date, the handshake remains a symbol of two opposing parties coming together in agreement. All this was achieved without a peacekeeping force, proving that it is never necessary to send soldiers to help end war. How can soldiers who are only trained to fight end a war? Isn't it logical to assume that the only thing they will achieve is to prolong the fighting? The way to stop violence is to send people with a proven track record of diplomacy and statesmanship to help warring parties come together. Any solution that involves men with guns is not a solution but an excuse to achieve some hidden agendas. It is time we questioned those who continue to spread this myth and firmly reject the false narrative of the peacekeeping force.

The myth of the righteous West

Closely related to the lie of the peacekeeping force is the myth of the righteous West. This is the idea that the West is a force for good, only interested in spreading freedom and democracy around the world. The West portrays itself as civilized and modern while the rest of the world is portrayed as backward, savage, undeveloped and in need of saving and civilizing. Hence the cliché of the white saviour. The idea that the West is a civilising force on the planet has been used as an excuse for everything from the colonization and oppression of people around the world to the brutal crusades of the catholic church. The West has done such a stellar job of spreading this worldview that today it is still the predominant worldview held by most people. Most people believe that everything the West does is good, from its humanitarian activities to its intervention in other countries' affairs. The truth, however, is quite different from the propaganda.

The humanitarian activities carried out by the West would be admirable, were it not for the fact that the wars and poverty they supposedly try to resolve were created by the same West. The West has been guilty of plundering the wealth and natural resources of many countries around the world. The West is also the largest manufacturer and supplier of the weapons that cause much of the instability on the planet. As if this was not enough, the West is today involved in the destabilization of countries around the world, from Africa to South America to Asia. Why? Because a stable world would not be in the best interest of the West. The West needs the world to be unstable and constantly at war as this is the only way they will have a ready market for their endless supply of weapons. They keep corrupt governments in power as this is the only way they can extract wealth from these countries. If the wars and instability on the planet were to end today, the West would probably become bankrupt or at the very least need to reinvent itself.

Although people by now should know better, we continue to fall for the lie that the West is a righteous force. We believe them when they say that they intervene in countries to spread freedom and democracy. We believed them when they said that they invaded Iraq to find weapons of mass destruction. We believed them when they said that they invaded Libya to remove a brutal tyrant. We believed them when they said that they invaded Syria to stop the use of chemical weapons. We continue to believe them today when they say that they are intervening in Ukraine to stop evil Putin. When will we stop holding on to this naïve worldview? When will we realize that the only purpose this worldview serves is to keep us silent while the West does whatever they want on the planet? When will we realize that the only thing the West is interested in is the total domination of the globe? If we could only understand that the West consistently strives to spread its hegemony, we would see through the many lies they feed us.   Right now, the world is reeling from unbearable inflation and a lack of food and fuel. The West is of course unwilling to take responsibility for the fact that our misery is a direct result of their actions. If anyone still thinks the West is righteous given what is happening today, then they seriously need to ask themselves just how completely propagandized they are.

Just to be clear, I do not blame the majority of Westerners for the problems we face on the planet as they are as much victims of their psychopathic leaders as everyone else. But they cannot escape responsibility for what their leaders are doing around the world, because their leaders act on their behalf and with their taxes. Therefore, they have a greater responsibility than everyone else on the planet for the actions of their leaders. It is not enough for them to live their lives, not bothered by what their governments are doing. The French people have to ask what their military is doing in West Africa. The American people have to ask why their government has military bases around the planet and why their government is sending tonnes of weapons to Ukraine. Every citizen in the West has to demand that their governments stop their nefarious activities around the planet. We see Westerners pressuring their governments all the time for social change, from abortion rights to gay rights. If their governments continue to be engaged in violent activities around the world, it is because the citizens do not care enough to make them stop.

Survival of the fittest

Survival of the fittest is an ideology that originated in the 19th century as a way of explaining Charles Darwin's theory of natural selection. Unfortunately, this ideology has been used as a justification for everything from eugenics to laissez-faire economics, war and racism. This theory has been used to justify the idea that society should be ruled by a small group of elites who are more intelligent than the masses. When taken to the extreme, this theory has been used to justify the killing and sterilization of the "less fit" members of society through the eugenics movement. The eugenics movement took off in the early 20th century in Europe and the United States, with several states passing laws that required the sterilization of those who were considered unfit. It should be obvious to everyone that nobody has a right to decide whether another human being is fit to live or reproduce, but clearly, it was not obvious to the people who were behind these ideas. It was not until the Nazis took the ideology to its natural conclusion and started killing people who were considered unfit that the world finally woke up to how truly evil this ideology is. Hopefully, this is a lesson that humanity will not quickly forget about the dangers of flirting with ideologies that allow certain people to decide who is and is not worthy to live.

The ideology of survival of the fittest is behind the laissez-faire model of economics in which the government avoids regulating the economy and leaves everyone to fight it out among themselves. According to this theory, this is the natural order of things and it is the way God intended the world to work. But the effect of this ideology is the situation we now find ourselves in whereby a small group of elites own almost all the world's wealth while the rest of humanity is left to share out the remaining crumbs. This same mindset is out-pictured on the planet with a few countries having most of the world's wealth while others have to live in abject poverty. The fact that we accept this state of affairs means that we have been deceived and completely blinded by the ideology of survival of the fittest. Many people do not see anything wrong with the majority of the world's population living in abject poverty because they assume there must be something wrong with them if they cannot thrive like everyone else. We do not see why anyone should help them come up as we feel it is their responsibility to pull themselves up. What we may not realize is that the way the world is structured, it would be impossible for everyone to thrive. It is not just a question of some people not putting in enough effort. We have people who labour every day from morning to evening but remain poor. The simple reason is that the majority of the world's wealth is being hoarded by a few elites. It doesn't matter how much we fight over the remaining crumbs; we will always have some people going without. Even in the so-called wealthy countries, most people do not live in true wealth but exist from pay check to pay check. They are as much slaves of the elites as we in the global south are slaves of the wealthier nations. The only way the elites can get us to go along with this cruel state of affairs is by making us believe that those who don't do well are simply lazy. Westerners despise people in less developed countries not realizing that they themselves are as much victims of the elites as everyone else.

The same ideology of survival of the fittest is used to justify racism and we continue to live in a world that is completely affected by this idea.

We may try to hide the fact that the majority of people on earth are under the influence of racist ideas, but the truth is self-evident in the way the world is structured. We cannot hide the truth from ourselves because whatever is hidden in our subconscious simply manifests as the reality we live in. How can we say that the world is not under the influence of racism when it is clear for anyone to see that the poorest parts of the world are the ones where black and brown people live while the wealthiest parts are the ones where white people live? How did this state of affairs come to be? Is this a natural phenomenon created by God or is it the result of our beliefs becoming manifest? God teaches us justice and love for our neighbours and if we were to create a world that is based on Godly principles, then we would not have the sorry state of affairs we see out-pictured today.

When it comes to war, the ideology of survival of the fittest has been used by certain nations to justify their violent activities on the planet. The United States is a prime example of a country that believes in this ideology. It believes that it has a right to project its strength everywhere on the planet and bully everyone into doing whatever it wants. Any country that tries to resist the United States is met with destabilisation and outright war. This is one of the reasons the planet is forever in a state of unrest. It is due to the activities of one rogue nation that is completely convinced of its right to rule the world, simply because it has the biggest arsenal of weapons and the strongest economy. But we know that historically, this attitude eventually leads to collapse as the country becomes more and more corrupt. We are seeing this happening in real-time today as the United States starts its inevitable decline and becomes more and more unpredictable and desperate to hold on to its fading glory. What would help this country would be to use its wealth as a force for good to help lift other weaker nations. Instead of flooding the world with weapons, it should flood the world with love. Instead of trying to raise itself above everyone else, it should try to lift others to its level and in that way, it will end up raising higher itself.

Is a world without war possible?

Most of us have grown up believing that war is a natural part of life on this planet. We have grown up seeing wars on the news and seeing war depicted in the entertainment industry. If you ask the average person whether it is possible to have a world without war, they will probably tell you that it is impossible. War has been so normalized on this planet that it is almost impossible for most of us to imagine a world without war. War is such a normal part of life on this planet that it almost seems naïve to imagine that one day we could have a world without war. The problem with this attitude is that unless people can imagine something, they will not even begin to put any effort towards it. Much of the progress we have made as human beings has been because someone imagined that life could be different. The reason we have aeroplanes is that someone imagined that it should be possible for human beings to fly. Whatever efforts they made at first must have seemed bizarre and unusual to most people and it is likely they endured the ridicule of many people. But their belief kept them going until they finally found a solution. We all know how far this technology has come today. None of this would have been possible if everyone had assumed that if God wanted human beings to fly, he would have given us wings.

If we look at the situation as it is on the planet today, it is quite possible to assume that human beings were always meant to be at war with each other. We could assume that if God had intended for us to live at peace with each other, he would not have created us with the differences that cause us to be at war with each other. But that would be a serious misunderstanding of how God intended us to live on this planet. God expects us to overcome whatever challenges we encounter and use them as a stepping stone to come up higher. No challenge should be endured for all eternity. That is why we look for cures for diseases and solutions to engineering problems. That is why we are not living in caves today. Human beings can always make life better for themselves. War is a challenge we are currently faced with and we need to see it as such. As long as we continue accepting it as a way of life, then it will never go away. But if we decide to approach it like any other problem that can be overcome, we will gradually climb out of this darkness that has enveloped us for too long.

The vast majority of human beings only go to war because we buy the elites' false narratives without question. We believe that our neighbours are a threat to us. We believe that they want to take away our freedom and democracy. We believe that God wants us to forcefully convert people to our religion. All these are lies we have come to believe after centuries of deception. Once you take away the deception, you realize that war is completely unnecessary. If there were no psychopaths constantly pushing people to go to war, we would not have wars on this planet. We need to start imagining a world without war as a possibility and reject every narrative that says that we have to go to war for any reason at all. There is no reason whatsoever for anyone to go to war with anyone. Once we stop listening to the worst people among us who keep saying that war is inevitable, then we can start remaking our planet into the kind of planet we want to live in.

Chapter 6
A Spiritual Perspective

Who is the man who delights in life, who desires to see good days? Keep your tongue from evil and your lips from deceitful speech. Turn away from evil and do good; seek peace and pursue it. The eyes of the LORD are on the righteous, and His ears are inclined to their cry. But the face of the LORD is against those who do evil, to wipe out all memory of them from the earth.

Psalms 34:12-16

Most of us believe in God, a higher power or some kind of supernatural being. We believe that we are not here by some accident of nature but were created by an intelligent creator. If we were created by an intelligent creator, then surely, he must have had some purpose for placing us on this planet. Is it logical to believe that God created billions of human beings and placed them on the planet without some sort of purpose for creating them? Why did God place us on this planet? The simple answer is that God placed us on this planet for growth. We are not the result of random events, although this is the view that has been taught to us through our education systems. Once you get people to believe that they are the result of random events, then they stop seeing themselves as having a higher purpose. We have been told that we are animals, no different from other animals except in our level of intelligence. No wonder it then becomes possible to convince human beings to kill each other, because they view themselves as just another animal species. We have been deceived into giving up the understanding of ourselves as spiritual beings and instead to view ourselves as animals. The truth is that we are not animals and we could not be further from the animal species because we have self-awareness. By denying our spiritual identity, we allow ourselves to be treated as bodies that can be sent to war in the never-ending quest for power and resources.

We go through many experiences in life, some positive and some negative, but the underlying principle is that every experience is an opportunity for growth. From the moment we are born to the day we die, life is a series of experiences that are meant to lead to our growth or self-transcendence. In school, we learn the basics that enable us to become self-reliant. Marriage and parenthood are yet other opportunities for us to learn and grow. The point I am trying to make is that life is about growth, self-transcendence and bettering ourselves. Contrast this with war, which is the senseless destruction of life and property. War is the exact opposite of what God placed us on this planet to do. War has absolutely no value in that we don't learn anything from it. All it brings out is savagery and brutality, qualities that do not in any way contribute to the growth of society. It should be obvious to everyone that war is not God's plan for humanity. The psychopaths among us will naturally not accept such a view of life because they believe that they have a right to do whatever they want. As long as we keep allowing the worst people among us to determine the path we take, we will keep defaulting to destructive, meaningless activities that do not in any way lead to our growth.

One of the lessons we are meant to be learning is how to manage our free will. Free will does not mean doing whatever we want and then turning around and blaming God when we make a mess. God has given us this planet as a platform for our growth - if we destroy it because we are unwilling to learn how to responsibly use our free will, then we have no one to blame but ourselves. While God has given us free will to choose whatever experiences we want to have on the planet, surely we cannot believe that war is one of the experiences God wants for us. War takes us backwards and destroys our creative achievements. If we keep defaulting to war, then we get lost in a cycle of creating and destroying that stops the very process of growth that we are supposed to be undergoing. We have not been abandoned here by God as some would have us believe but were placed here by a loving God who would have us use our creativity to grow and become better versions of ourselves. How do we become better versions of ourselves? We do so by being creative and constantly building on our creativity. This is the true purpose of life.

Love Your Neighbour as Yourself

For the entire law is fulfilled in keeping this one command: "Love your neighbour as yourself.

Galatians 5:14

Our planet is inhabited by people from different cultures, languages, races, ways of life, and so on. What is the one thing that can bring us all together and allow us to live in harmony? It is love for one another. If we saw each other as human beings deserving of love and compassion, we would never attack each other and attempt to destroy each other. The one ingredient that is lacking in the world today is love. For too long, we have been taught that our differences make us superior or inferior to each other, that some races are more deserving than others of living lives of wealth and abundance and that some cultures are savage and primitive while others are civilized and advanced. And yet the reality is that no culture is inherently superior to any other, just as no race is inherently superior to any other. All of us are on a journey of evolving into better versions of ourselves. The people who consider themselves advanced had to start from somewhere to get where they are today. The people who appear to be backward are also on the same journey of transcending themselves to become better versions of themselves. The reality is that all human beings are created equal and deserve to live lives of dignity. It is only when we love others as ourselves that we can treat them the way we would like to be treated.

In order to wage war against other people, the one thing we have to suppress is our love for our fellow human beings. We have to deny their humanity and instead see them as an inferior species that we do not need to treat the way human beings should be treated. That is why the first step in waging war is to dehumanise the "enemy", creating fear, anger and hatred toward them. When these emotions reach a tipping point, then people can be convinced to take up arms and destroy the "enemy". Without this initial step, people would simply have no interest or desire to attack anyone. The United States has spent the last few decades creating fear and animosity toward Russia and China. The American people have unfortunately bought this lie, even though Russians and Chinese people do not pose any threat to them. The only people who are threatened by the Russians and Chinese are the elites with their endless quest for global domination. In their quest for "full spectrum dominance", they are willing to go to any lengths and that is why we are increasingly hearing talk of a war between the United States and its allies and China/Russia. No one wants such a war because it would mean the annihilation of life on this planet. And for what? So that a few psychopaths can hold on to the illusion that they are the most powerful people on earth? Why should we stand by and allow them to manipulate us into hating each other and killing each other? How long will the people in the West allow themselves to be used as pawns? Only love for their neighbours can bring about a change of heart that will allow them to see others as their brothers and sisters. Only then can we hope to heal our planet and start a new era of peace.

Turn the Other Cheek

But I say to you, do not resist an evil person; but whoever slaps you on your right cheek, turn the other to him also.

Matthew 5:39

Anyone familiar with this bible verse will also be familiar with the inner feeling of tension or doubt that it causes. Turn the other cheek? As in allow someone to not only slap me but timidly offer them my other cheek as well? This goes against everything we have been taught. Everyone knows that you are supposed to fight back when attacked. Everyone knows that it is cowardly to let someone kick you around without responding with equal or greater force. Everyone knows that you have to eat or be eaten, kill or be killed. That is how the world works. At least that is what we have been led to believe. We are supposed to be hard, assertive and able to take care of ourselves. Jesus can't have meant what he said. But on the other hand, when we look at the state the world is in today, where did this philosophy get us? We live in a world full of unimaginable brutality and violence. How can we believe that even *more* aggression is the answer? It doesn't matter how aggressive you are, there will always be someone willing to go further than you possibly could. The only way to end the cycle of aggression is to not fight back. That is the lesson we learnt from Mahatma Gandhi. And that is the lesson Jesus was trying to impart to a world that believes in violence and revenge as the only means of survival. If people were to take the extraordinary step of turning the other cheek, then we would see an end to the violence currently plaguing the planet.

What is the one reason that stops people from heeding Jesus' words to turn the other cheek? It is the idea that this is a cowardly or shameful thing to do. The reason we have so much violence on this planet is that everyone believes that they have to fight back otherwise they will be considered cowards. When a country goes to war, everyone is supposed to show eagerness to fight. Everyone is supposed to set aside their normal, rational thinking that tells them that life is precious and should be preserved and instead be eager to have their life cut short on the battlefield. How did we become so brainwashed that we would be willing to set aside our most basic instinct of self-preservation in order to fight wars that do not benefit us in any way? Why can't we see through this deception? What is so admirable or brave about reacting with violence to provocation? The truth is that turning the other cheek is a sign of strength, not cowardice. Resisting the urge to lash out at the person provoking us is one of the hardest acts of self-control. Unfortunately, we live in an upside-down world in which aggression is praised while gentleness is reviled, violence is glorified while self-control is mocked and arrogance is respected while humility is despised. That is why Jesus' words appear so strange to us today. We cannot imagine a world where gentleness, self-control and humility are the norms. But it is possible to create such a world. We can create a new, peaceful world that we are all happy to live in. We have the power to do so; we only need to change the beliefs that brought us where we are today.

If you feel an inner discomfort at the idea of turning the other cheek, it means you are a victim of the false ideologies that dominate our planet today. Take time to examine your beliefs and ask yourself why you believe what you believe. Most of us when confronted with Jesus' words simply dismiss them as impractical. But these words could change our world if we understood how powerful they are. They go against everything we have been taught, but then again look where that got us. Look at the state of the world today. Is anyone happy with the current state of the planet? If not, then we have the responsibility to try something new. After all, it is said that insanity is continuing to do the same thing and expecting different results. Jesus' words are exactly what is needed to heal this planet of the endless cycle of violence and war.

Forgiveness

Bear with each other and forgive one another if any of you has a grievance against someone. Forgive as the Lord forgave you.

Colossians 3:13

Many peoples on this planet have been in conflict with each other for generations. Some of these grievances have been going on for so long that no one even remembers how they began. Take for example the conflict between the Palestinians and the Israelis. These people have been at war with each other for eons. It doesn't appear as if the conflict is going to end any time soon. Why should generations of human beings continue fighting each other over strips of land that have no special value? In the past, people thought they needed more and more territory, but today most countries have settled down and accepted their borders no matter how those borders came to be. Africa, which was curved up by colonialists who did not have any regard for the history or culture of the inhabitants is a good example of this. In the end, it doesn't matter who took whose land and who was there first. The fact is, you are all here now and you somehow have to co-exist with each other. What was done was done. The Palestinians understandably feel that they are being treated unfairly, but if you look at the history of most people on the planet today, everyone was treated unfairly at some point. History is full of territories being taken forcefully by a more aggressive force and we cannot continue forever bemoaning this fact. There is a place for acceptance and for moving on. Otherwise, you end up with grievances that go on for centuries. The Palestinians have to accept the reality that a more aggressive force came and forcefully occupied their land and there is no removing them from there. They can continue fighting for generations or they can sit down together and agree on a sensible solution that will result in peace. After all, we all found ourselves living on this planet which we did not create; we cannot claim inherent ownership of the land we live on. Why fight over something you do not and cannot own?   Naturally, the Israelis need to end their aggressive stance and humbly come to the table to negotiate.

Part of the reason why people are so unwilling to let go of grievances is that we have been taught that it is weak to let someone walk all over us. We have been taught that we have to fight back, we have to resist the enemy and we have to stand up for ourselves. And of course, there is a place for that. Sometimes we have to resist but we have to do so in a *non-violent* way. Violent resistance is not true resistance because we have to stoop to the same level as the person we are supposedly resisting. If someone does you wrong and you repay them with wrong, what is the difference between the two of you? Aren't you just as evil as the person you are resisting? Are you any different from the violent person you are resisting if you have to resort to violence? We are supposed to be evolving, transcending ourselves and becoming better versions of ourselves. We cannot continue resolving issues the way our forefathers used to do it. That is why the subtitle of this book is "Transcending a primitive practice that has no place in the modern world". We have to move away from the way things were done in the past and find new, civilised ways of resolving issues. It is not cowardly to forgive and accept that whatever happened in the past happened. Forgive the wrong that was done to you and allow the wound to heal.

Today, forgiveness is a forgotten virtue. Letting someone "get away with it" is a sign of weakness. But the truth is that we all wrong someone at some point in life. No one can claim that they have never wronged anyone. For people to live in harmony, there must be forgiveness. You must forgive others just the same way you need them to forgive you when you wrong them. Otherwise, how would we live with others? The idea that forgiveness is a sign of weakness is completely baseless. The same applies to nations, not just to individuals. If one nation feels wronged by another, the way to go about resolving the issue is not to shoot first and ask questions later. It is to be willing to sit down with the party that wronged you, express your views and find a way forward. How can we hope to live at peace with each other if everyone operates with hubris and arrogance? We have to be willing to forgive each other and let go of perceived wrongs just the same way we need others to forgive us and let go of whatever wrongs we may have done to them.

Do not kill

Thus says the Lord, "Do justice and righteousness, and deliver the one who has been robbed from the power of his oppressor. Also do not mistreat or do violence to the stranger, the orphan, or the widow; and do not shed innocent blood in this place.

* **Jeremiah 22:3** *

The sixth commandment "thou shalt not kill" is straightforward and unambiguous but somehow, we still find ways to justify killing on this planet. People kill others in the name of the same God who commands us not to kill. Many people have fallen for the lie that God sometimes allows us to disregard this commandment when circumstances call for it. For example, if someone attempts to kill you then it is okay to kill them first. Or when it comes to defending your country, it is okay to kill. But the truth is that life is a gift from God and no one has the right to take away anyone else's life no matter what the circumstances. This is one of the most fundamental laws on this planet. Taking someone's life results in karma that must be repaid either in this lifetime or in future lifetimes. The reason many people think that you can break God's laws and get away with it is that they do not understand that karma does not return immediately. Just because no flash of lightning strikes you dead when you break God's laws doesn't mean that you got away with it. People need to understand that life is an ongoing process that does not end when one leaves the body. This is a truth that has long been denied especially by the Christian religion. The denial of the reality of reincarnation is one reason people think that they are getting away with living life however they want. In truth, God cannot be mocked and whatever is hidden from man is not hidden from God. What goes around comes around, if not in this lifetime, then in subsequent lifetimes.

Killing is an act that most people instinctively know is unacceptable to God. This is written in our very DNA. So why have people allowed themselves to become manipulated into accepting the lie that it is okay to kill? Well, it takes a lot of effort to get human beings to kill and it just so happens that there are people who are very much invested in this. The violence we see on TV and in movies is one of the ways they achieve this. The gaming industry is another tool they use to get people used to the idea of violence and killing from an early age. To create soldiers that will suppress their instinct not to kill, you have to desensitise human beings to violence and teach them how to kill. Killing does not come naturally to human beings the way it does to predators. We have to be taught how to suppress our humanity and ignore God's laws to get us to kill. And the results of ignoring God's laws make themselves clear in the form of PTSD, depression and suicides that we see occurring in the military. Most human beings would not even know how to kill if it wasn't for the training they receive from the military. Why do you think the military has to keep people isolated from the rest of humanity while undergoing daily drills? This is how you kill their humanity. We also know of the usage of drugs during war, which is another way soldiers are desensitized to what they are doing. The sad part is that even after all the training and drugs, most soldiers still suffer immensely when they kill or watch their colleagues being killed. But nobody tells them that when they are being recruited. The military is made to sound like an honourable calling and a service to the community. To date, despite all the evidence to the contrary, many people consider a career in the military to be a prestigious career. We even hear rumours of people paying huge bribes to join the military; but of course, this cannot be ascertained. Suffice it to say that the brainwashing has been most effective. The question is, when are we going to stop believing what we are told and instead follow God's eternal laws? This is the only path that can bring us true happiness. As long as we continue breaking God's laws, we will continue suffering the consequences, which include a planet that has become one big killing machine. The sooner we reject this deception the sooner we can restore sanity to this planet.

Diplomacy

If your brother or sister sins go and point out their fault, just between the two of you. If they listen to you, you have won them over. But if they will not listen, take one or two others along, so that 'every matter may be established by the testimony of two or three witnesses.'

Matthew 19:15-16

Diplomacy is the art of getting two or more parties to agree on a matter without resorting to violence. In the past, nations and tribes used to resolve their differences through violence, which is why history is littered with tales of nations conquering nations and tribes warring against each other. But as time went on, we discovered that conflicts do not have to lead to violence. We saw the sheer wastage of energy and resources that violence produced and we became tired of the violent way of resolving issues. Unfortunately, not everyone got tired of violence and we still have people today calling for violence at every opportunity. The warmongers among us who benefit from war will not allow us to enter a new, peaceful stage of the world's evolution. They continue sabotaging every effort at peace and pulling us back whenever we make any meaningful steps towards peace. The Russia-Ukraine war is a good example of their relentless efforts to keep the world in a state of war. It has become increasingly clear that NATO and the Western nations fronting it are not interested in diplomacy as a solution to the conflict. President Zelensky is nothing more than a puppet of the West and his actions simply reflect the wishes of the people controlling him. If it was not for the West sending weapons and mercenaries into Ukraine it is doubtful that the war would still be going on. At the very least, Ukraine would have been forced to go to the table to negotiate with the Russians. The hard-line stance that President Zelensky has taken is a reflection of the people behind him that are pushing for more war. NATO has reached that point in its existence where it is no longer relevant and therefore it has to create the very problems it was created to solve. Without war, there would be no need for NATO. Therefore, the very institution that was created to prevent war, if we can even believe that the people behind NATO were ever interested in peace, has now morphed into an institution that has to provoke wars to survive. It should be clear to everyone that this is the reason NATO cannot accept or encourage peaceful negotiations. It is quite hypocritical of the United States and its allies to keep talking about standing with Ukraine when they have not even sent representatives for talks between Ukraine and Russia. All they do is escalate the war by sending more weapons. Why aren't they interested in peace? Because peace is not profitable for them. Peace is only profitable and desirable to the rest of humanity but not to the people behind the war industry.

How can we strengthen diplomacy on this planet? The first thing we need to do is dismantle all institutions that serve no other purpose than to entrench the consciousness of war. NATO is a good example of such an institution, but there are many others including the United States Commands that are located on every continent. What purpose do these Commands serve other than to train people for war, look out for opportunities for war and keep the world on a permanent war footing? These should immediately be dismantled. What about the US military bases that are scattered across most countries on the planet? Why does the United States need to have so many military bases? Who exactly is threatening them? What is so special about the United States that they feel that everyone is out to get them? Is it maybe because of their nefarious activities around the world that are ironically supposed to keep the safe? These military bases need to be dismantled. And speaking of the United States' nefarious activities, the other institution that needs to be dismantled is the CIA. This must surely be one of the most evil institutions the world has ever seen. Not only is it involved in the destabilization of countries around the world, but it also commits unspeakable evils against the American people under the guise of scientific experiments. The crimes this institution has committed are simply unimaginable. But what would you expect from an organisation that took in the Nazis that were fleeing from Germany after the war (Operation Paperclip)?

The second thing that needs to be done to strengthen diplomacy is to support institutions that promote peace around the world. These include the United Nations, regional bodies such as the African Union, embassies and foreign ministries. Countries must continue to train and place more emphasis on diplomats as an integral part of their foreign relations. As the world becomes more oriented toward the military, the art of diplomacy is in decline. Powerful nations that should be at the forefront of diplomatic efforts such as the United States are now more focused on military might as the sole solution to all problems. In the past, the United States was at the centre of peace initiatives such as the one between Israel and Palestine. Today, this is no longer the case. They could take a leaf from China which is using its influence to help lift the rest of the world through its Belt and Road initiative. We see China's influence soaring as the United States' influence wanes. This clearly shows that it is not the size or strength of the military that determines your influence on the world stage but how the world perceives you. The United States must understand that no civilization can last forever, especially once it becomes corrupt.

Last but not least, we need to understand that as long as private corporations exist that profit from war, we will always have wars on this planet. We need to systematically dismantle the private sector actors that are behind the wars on this planet. These people fund the think tanks that orient us towards war, they act behind the scenes and use their dark money to influence policy and they are behind the efforts to desensitize humanity to violence. These are the people who shape our worldview when it comes to war. Without this key factor, no one would support war. We need to see through their deception and reject a world that is created to sustain and expand their power. We need to stop being naïve in thinking that the world we live in "just is". Our world is being shaped by powerful forces that work in the shadows, out of sight, creating the chaos we experience every day. Unless we open our eyes and see what is happening, we will continue being their slaves and doing their bidding without us knowing that we are being controlled. The next chapters will look at our personal and collective responsibility when it comes to ending war on this planet.

Chapter 7
Personal Responsibility

One of the most unfortunate things about war is that the people who fight are ordinary people who somehow become convinced that they need to take up arms against an external enemy who presents an existential threat. Wars are not fought by the elites who pass the laws and make the decisions that send people to the battlefield. They are not fought by the politicians who decide that a certain country presents a threat that needs to be neutralized or by the journalists who write opinion pieces glorifying war. They are not fought by the think tanks that come up with slick arguments in support of war or by the weapons manufacturers who churn out the instruments of death. They are fought by ordinary people who are brainwashed into blindly and unquestioningly believing what they are told. The soldiers who sacrifice their lives on the battlefield are unfortunately seen as nothing more than a mass of disposable bodies that are used to forward the agendas of the elites. Their lives mean nothing to the people who send them out to die. They are treated as nothing more than numbers, not people with families, dreams, ambitions and a higher purpose. The death of a soldier is not viewed as a tragic and avoidable loss of life but as an expected consequence of war. Since the work of a soldier is to fight an enemy who is just as determined as they are to kill before getting killed, the death of a soldier is deemed a normal and acceptable part of war. While the death of civilians is treated as regrettable and to be avoided at all costs, the death of a soldier is treated as if it is unimportant. This dehumanization is what allows wars to continue and we have all been brainwashed into accepting this as normal.

War is nothing more than a scam that makes billions of dollars for certain people. This is something that is acknowledged even by former soldiers who connect the dots once they see the reality of war and how meaningless it is. When they compare the propaganda they were fed during training with the reality on the battlefield, those who are capable of reflection usually end up with a moral injury as they discover that the ideals they thought they were fighting for are nothing more than a mirage that completely vanishes on the battlefield. Unfortunately, this reality of war is rarely talked about in the mainstream media that is completely captured by the war complex. The ordinary person is only exposed to the narrative that calls for more and more war and rarely gets to hear any opposing ideas. The only way we will come out of this rabbit hole is by people taking responsibility for themselves and thinking for themselves. We have to reject the idea that we are nothing more than bodies that can be used to serve the agendas of the elites.

Should you join the military?

If people knew the truth about the war industry, no one would ever volunteer to join the military, which is why they go to such great lengths to hide the reality of it. The military is sold as a noble institution and working for the military is portrayed as a heroic service to your country, an act of valour which protects our freedom and democracy. In the West, the military is supposedly the institution that guarantees Western hegemony, which in turn maintains the so-called "rules-based order". It is assumed that this rules-based order is what we all want, even though no one ever tells us what these rules are, who wrote them and why we should obey them. A military "career" - if killing people can be considered a career - is seen as prestigious and lucrative, with benefits that include travel to various exotic locations around the world. But nobody tells the young men and women who join the military exactly what they are signing up for. Before you decide to join the military, you need to understand that it is not an adventure that opens doors for you to explore the world and earn good money while you're at it. It is important to consider all the facts, not just what the PR machine churns out. The thing no one mentions when they carry out their recruitment exercises is that joining the military is akin to signing a contract with the devil. You are committing not only to killing people when called upon to do so but also sacrificing your own life in case you end up on the wrong side of the barrel. Before signing such a contract, ask yourself if you are okay with that. It's not just about the money and the adventure but about the deeper questions that arise from such a commitment. Is killing people something you agree with or would even think of doing in the normal course of life? If not, why sign up for a career that requires you to do just that? Such ethical questions are never addressed during the recruitment exercise. This is about taking responsibility for yourself and the decisions you make. You cannot wait until the day you find yourself on the battlefield to start asking questions. When you join the military, you need to understand what you are signing up for. You have to see beyond the enticements and see clearly what you will be getting yourself into. Do not be fooled by the rosy picture of travelling the world and earning a good living for yourself and your family. At some point, you *will* be called upon to fight, meaning you *will* be required to kill other people who are also trying to kill you. This is what the military is at its core. If you have watched a war movie, you know that the battlefield is a horrible mess of blood and gore. Why would you consciously subject yourself to this? Why would you volunteer for this when no one is holding a gun to your head forcing you to do so? Is any amount of money worth the psychological suffering you will experience after seeing the reality of what war entails? Are you ready to give up your limbs in service to someone else's delusional and insane agenda? Because the idea that war is a noble service to society is pure lunatic ideology. Everything they tell us to justify war is pure propaganda and lies. We have been manipulated into believing that there is an enemy out there trying to destroy us when in reality the enmity is dreamt up by the very people who ask us to fight. It is all for their benefit.

If you are lucky enough to escape death or bodily injuries on the battlefield, you need to consider the psychological wounds you are likely to suffer once you experience war. Killing does not come naturally to most human beings and hence you cannot escape the consequences of going against your God-given nature. When you kill others, you may tell yourself that you have done nothing wrong because you have been taught to justify evil for the "greater good". But the reality is that when you hurt others, you are hurting yourself first and foremost because we are all connected. We have been taught to see ourselves not as spiritual beings but as slightly advanced animals. But this is not true. We are extensions of our creator and we are all connected at inner levels. This is why many soldiers simply fall apart when they leave the battlefield. We know that many soldiers suffer from depression, anxiety and post-traumatic stress disorder (PTSD) when they leave the battlefield. They experience guilt, grief, regret and inner torment for their part in the war. Many of them experience moral injury as a result of the things they saw on the battlefield. These are the real effects of their attempt to deny their spiritual nature and the spiritual nature of those they harmed who are also created in God's image. The resulting trauma is undeniable, which is why we have high levels of suicide among soldiers. The military of course pretends to study the cause of these suicides while ignoring the obvious cause which is that human beings are not wired to be killers.

The other thing no one ever tells you when they recruit you into the military is that sexual assault and harassment are rampant within the military. Why would you join an institution where your chances of being sexually assaulted are much higher than if you stayed out? Why would you take an action that is against your own self-interest? The military is a den of the worst human beings on earth and you need to be aware of this before you sign up. The majority of people who join the military are decent people who unfortunately become deceived by the PR machine into believing that they are serving their country. But we would be naïve not to expect that sociopaths would be attracted to a career in the military because it offers them the opportunity to harm people and get paid for it. Therefore, before you join the military, be aware that you are joining an institution that is home to some of the worst people on the planet. You can expect behaviours that are normally associated with sociopaths to be rampant in the military. Before you sign that contract, ask yourself what the consequences will be for you personally. Forget what everyone tells you. Once you join the military, you will be on your own facing the consequences of your choices. There will be no one to blame for whatever happens on the battlefield because no one forced you to join the military. And if you think you will be able to quit if you don't like it, think again. The military is not an institution you can simply walk away from like any other institution. You don't get to quit just because you don't like it. You will have to see your contract through to the end. Therefore, think twice, thrice, a hundred times before you decide to join the military.

Change your worldview

To change the planet, we have to start by changing ourselves. If you believe that killing is sometimes justified, it means that you have taken on the fallen belief system that the end justifies the means. This belief makes it possible for anyone to justify anything and does not take into account any higher truths. The truth is that no one has the right to take someone else's life no matter what the circumstances. The aggressive people among us of course cannot imagine a world in which one responds with anything other than violence when provoked. They cannot conceive of human beings as spiritual beings with a higher purpose which precludes killing. Their mindset reduces human beings to animals whose sole purpose is survival and who therefore must do anything they can to survive, including killing. But we know that human beings are extensions of the creator and therefore we have to live by higher laws. The creator does not make any exceptions. When confronted with evil, we have to turn the other cheek otherwise we become no better than the evil we are supposedly resisting. Unless we are completely convinced of this truth, we will always feel that violence is sometimes justified.

The idea that killing is sometimes justified is a slippery slope because how do we determine where to draw the line? Do we draw the line when someone attacks us personally? Do we draw the line when our loved ones are attacked? Do we draw the line when our country is attacked? If you accept that killing is sometimes justified, you might as well accept that killing is *always* justified because no one ever kills without some form of justification. Who is to say whether one person's justification is better than someone else's? In the end, the only valid response is that killing is *never* justified. We will never eliminate war on this planet while still believing that killing is sometimes justified. We need to live life according to God's higher laws, not the fallen worldview that is prevalent on the planet. The key is for more and more people to be able to see this truth because the planet is currently completely immersed in the idea that killing is sometimes justified. This idea keeps us trapped in a cycle of recurring violence and war. Your responsibility, therefore, is to resolve any wrong beliefs you may hold regarding killing, violence and war. As more and more people let go of the wrong belief system, we will start to see a change on the planet.

Raise your awareness

One of the biggest problems we face concerning war is that most ordinary people simply feel that it has nothing to do with them. We are programmed to believe that such topics are best left to the experts and that we have nothing to contribute. The so-called "experts", unfortunately, only lead us in one direction which is more war. Their only qualification, in reality, is that they are the most aggressive people on the planet and therefore their voices are the loudest. These people speak out aggressively and authoritatively about war, making everyone else feel as if they have nothing important to say. We are made to feel as if our opinions do not matter. Our opinions are made to look naïve and uninformed, so most of us simply lose interest and stop focusing on such issues, leaving the "experts" to say whatever they want. The reality is that war is not a complicated subject that the average person cannot understand. The reason we are made to feel like we don't understand this subject is that the logic used to justify war is fallen logic, where good is made to appear evil and evil is made to appear good. As an example, in the Russia-Ukraine war, we are told that the West is sending massive amounts of weapons to Ukraine to support freedom and democracy in that country. This doesn't make sense. We know logically that sending weapons to Ukraine only worsens and prolongs the war. We are also told that the West is leading an economic offensive to punish Russia, even though we can see that the sanctions are only causing suffering to the West and the entire planet. This action is completely illogical. Because the logic used to justify war does not follow common sense, we are made to feel that it is too complicated for the average person to understand. If anyone attempts to challenge this logic, they are viciously attacked and accused of all manner of things, which serves the purpose of silencing dissent and discouraging people from expressing their opinions for fear of being attacked. This is the main reason why the topic of war is dominated by the most aggressive voices that keep the planet permanently at war.

What is your responsibility in all this? It is to keep yourself informed on what is happening on the planet and trust your ability to understand and form an intelligent opinion. Read extensively on the wars that are currently taking place and find out what the issues are. Use your common sense to form opinions and draw your own conclusions. You do not need to rely on the opinions of so-called "experts" because chances are that the opinions expressed by these experts are the opposite of what common sense dictates. The people currently in positions of authority making the most important decisions on the planet are the least qualified to do so which is why they must make whatever they do sound complicated. Anyone with common sense can understand whatever is happening on the planet and make logical conclusions. Your responsibility is to educate yourself and use your logic to understand war. It is not too complicated: war = bad; peace = good. Anyone who tries to spin this any other way is outright lying to us and we have no obligation to listen to them.

Vote for politicians who are against war

In an ideal world, this is how democracy would work: we would vote for leaders who accurately reflect our aspirations and who would help bring about the kind of world we want to live in. Unfortunately, we do not live in an ideal world and what we have instead is a situation whereby leadership is about personal ambition and the desire for money and power. The people who aspire to leadership positions are more often than not driven by selfish motives that have nothing to do with the aspirations of the people. This is why every election cycle is followed by several years of disappointment and disillusionment that then lays the ground for the next election cycle. It is a wonder that people continue to vote time and time again. I wonder when people will simply get tired of this charade and stop showing up for elections. The idea that you must "cast your vote" to remove the current lot of leaders who have completely disappointed you and bring in fresh leaders who will meet your aspirations is nothing more than a farce. The whole election process is nothing more than an aspiring elite trying to remove the current elites and the ordinary people are just pawns in this game. I know this sounds cynical, but I have seen enough of this cycle to completely lose hope in the so-called democratic process. We are often manipulated into voting for the lesser evil, meaning we never actually get what we want. This is so normalized that it doesn't occur to us that we deserve better. We see this false democracy outplayed in many countries around the world, even in the so-called developed world. True democracy would involve voting for people who truly care about the things that are important to us and who translate our aspirations into reality.

Before voting for anyone, we must scrutinize what kind of person they are and what they stand for. We need to do some research which is not so hard with the internet. There is no excuse for voting for people who do not reflect our core values. We need to stop the current practice of voting along party lines. When we vote without knowing who we are voting for, we end up with aggressive, violent, corrupt, greedy war-mongers who lead us in directions we do not want to go. When we complain about bad leaders, we need to ask ourselves how they got there in the first place. We voted for them because we did not take the time to find out what kind of people we were voting for. With regard to war, it means voting for people who stand for peace, are non-aggressive and mature in their approach to politics. If someone aggressively attacks their opponent, it is a sign that they will respond aggressively to any provocation. These are the kinds of people who will be quick to lead the country to war. We need people who will respond with maturity and restraint in the face of provocation. We need to vote for people who have proven through their words and actions that they can be trusted to hold the fate of an entire nation in their hands. Our responsibility, therefore, is to do our homework before voting for any person. We need to reject the manipulation that forces us to make false choices that do not reflect what we want. It is better not to vote at all than to choose between two bad options. When we have leaders who are morally opposed to war and violence, we will stop seeing the kind of aggressive politics that are the norm on this planet. We need to remember that we live in an upside-down world where evil is good and good is evil. Therefore, voting for non-aggressive, morally upright people is often made to feel like the wrong thing to do. We have been taught to always go for the tough, aggressive and arrogant people because these are supposedly the "leadership qualities" we want. The former British Prime Minister Liz Truss stated just before her election that she would be willing to use nuclear weapons even if it meant the annihilation of the planet. She got a standing ovation for that comment and went on to win the election. Let that sink in for a second. In what world is this a sane position to hold? If we continue to choose such people as our leaders, is it any surprise that the world is heading towards nuclear war? Why do we act against our own self-interest by choosing such leaders? Only an insane person would be willing to start a nuclear war for *any* reason. This insane position supposedly shows her to be a tough leader suited for the task of leading a country. Unless we start seeing through these insane ideas and go in the opposite direction, we will continue choosing the wrong leaders and marching towards our destruction.

For most of us, as soon as elections are over, we quickly forget about politics and move on with our lives. We forget that elected leaders are supposed to represent our wishes and aspirations, meaning we have to keep them accountable once they are in office. This disconnect between the elected leaders and the electorate means that leaders quickly forget that they are there to serve the people and instead start pursuing their own interests and the interests of those who funded their campaigns. We, therefore, have a responsibility to keep track of what our leaders are doing. We need to know what laws are being debated in parliament and what our representatives are doing. The disconnect between the elected leaders and the electorate enables vested interests to lobby ceaselessly and influence the laws that are passed.   As citizens, our responsibility is to know who our representatives are, write letters expressing our views and pay them visits to make our views known. Those of us who are members of community groups such as church groups, estate associations, women's groups, etc, can use these groups to seek audience with the leaders and let them know what issues are important to them. Citizens of countries that are perennially at war have a responsibility to work extra hard to make their voices heard by their leaders. This is the only way leaders will stop sending their sons and daughters to fight endless wars. The citizens of these countries have to force their leaders to listen to them, otherwise, the leaders simply ignore the people's wishes and do whatever they want.

Let your voice be heard

One major problem facing the anti-war movement is that anti-war voices are not being heard. The aggressive narratives promoting war are the only ones being heard, mainly because such narratives are amplified by the mainstream media. As a result, even though most ordinary people do not want war, we continue having wars because our voices are not heard. Any anti-war voice is portrayed as naïve and unrealistic. Aggression and violence are normalized while being anti-war is made to look like a radical, unusual idea. The word "pacifist" is a dirty word in today's politics. The few voices that attempt to speak out against war are viciously attacked. This state of affairs has become so outrageous that even though we are one miscalculation away from nuclear war, no one seems interested in talking about peace. In the United Kingdom, it has become customary for anyone aspiring to become prime minister to unequivocally state that they are willing to use nuclear weapons. Nuclear war seems almost inevitable at this point. We remain silent because our world has been turned into a place where being aggressive is normal while being rational and cautious is abnormal. Those who oppose war must start to speak out otherwise our planet will be destroyed by people who have lost the ability to think rationally. Your responsibility, therefore, is to let your voice be heard. Speak out against war and be silent no more. If enough of us speak out, then we will eventually drown out the voices of the minority who are the loudest and most aggressive. There are many ways to speak out; you only need to be creative and do what you're comfortable with. You could start a blog in which you talk about war or you could write an article or two about war in an existing blog. You could write letters to your local politician expressing your views. You could write letters to your local newspaper. You could take it upon yourself to forward any interesting anti-war articles or videos to your social media groups.

As you speak out, remember to raise awareness about the prospect of nuclear war we are currently facing. We are in an extremely precarious position but the world doesn't seem to notice. We have unfortunately been lulled into a false sense of security by the myth of Mutually Assured Destruction (MAD), which is nothing more than a lie that keeps us passive. We have been led to believe that nuclear war can never happen because no one would be insane enough to risk mutually assured destruction. But we know for a fact that we have psychopaths in positions of power who would not hesitate to destroy the entire planet if pushed to a corner. We know that many elites today are building underground bunkers in preparation for some sort of apocalypse. Why do you think that is? What do they know that the rest of us don't? We must understand that the ruling elites do not see themselves as one with the rest of us, which is why they would prepare underground bunkers to protect themselves while not caring about the rest of us. Rather than do the sensible thing which is to use their power, wealth and influence to avert such a catastrophe, what they are doing instead is preparing to burrow underground like the rats they are while the rest of us are destroyed. This is the mentality these people have and they are the ones currently controlling the planet. Going by their behaviour, I would say that nuclear war is imminent. As long as the world remains silent under the false belief that nuclear war could never happen, we are simply sleepwalking towards our collective annihilation. Therefore, make it a part of your speaking-out efforts to talk about the potential for nuclear war and the need to ban nuclear weapons from the planet.

Support organisations that promote peace

One of the most practical things you could do to support peace and bring an end to war is to support organisations that promote peace. How do you support such organisations? By donating to them, taking part in their activities, signing their petitions and spreading their messages to other people. The idea is to do something, however small to support these organisations.

Below is a list of anti-war organisations you could consider supporting:

International:

- Beyond War
- International Campaign to Abolish Nuclear Weapons
- International Fellowship of Reconciliation
- International Peace Bureau
- International Physicians for the Prevention of Nuclear War
- Nobel Women's Initiative
- The Non-Violence Project
- World Beyond War
- World Peace Council
- Women's International League for Peace and Freedom

Africa:

- Anti-War Coalition

Asia:

- Peace Now
- National Council for Peace

Europe:

- German Peace Society
- International League of Peace
- League of Peace and Freedom
- Movement for a Non-violent Alternative
- Union pacifiste de France
- Groupe d'action et de résistance à la militarisation
- Mouvement pour le désarmement, la paix et la liberté
- Campaign for Nuclear Disarmament
- Peace Pledge Union
- Peace Society
- Stop the War Coalition

United States:

- American Peace Mobilization
- American Peace Society
- Antiwar.com
- Campus Antiwar Network
- Code Pink: Women for Peace
- National War Tax Resistance Coordinating Committee
- Peace Alliance
- The World Can't Wait
- United for Peace and Justice
- Veterans for Peace
- Win Without War
- Women's Peace Society
- Women's Peace Union

Canada:

- Canadian Peace Alliance
- Canadian Peace Congress

Religious:

- American Friends Service Committee
- Anglican Pacifist Fellowship
- Catholic Association for International Peace
- Christian Peace Conference
- Episcopal Peace Fellowship
- Fellowship of Reconciliation
- Lutheran Peace Fellowship
- Methodist Peace Fellowship
- Pentecostals & Charismatics for Peace & Justice
- Presbyterian Peace Fellowship
- Buddhist Peace Fellowship

Before we leave this chapter, I ask you to take a moment right now to decide what you want to do to help reduce war on the planet. The only way war ends on this planet is if a critical mass of people sees through the lies that have perpetuated war on this planet. This is how a new era of peace on this planet will begin. Your responsibility is to do at least one thing to help raise the planet. It doesn't have to be a big thing. It could be as simple as going to one of the websites of the organisations listed above *right now* and finding out more about what they do. It could be as simple as going to a local news website *right now* and writing a letter to the editor stating your opposition to an ongoing war. It could be as simple as writing an article on your blog *right now*. If you have more resources or time, you could contribute *right now* to an anti-war organisation or register to take part in their activities. Whatever you can do, commit to doing it *right now*, today, not tomorrow. No effort is too small or wasted. The world will not change by one person doing a great thing but by many people doing small things that collectively add up to a big thing.

Chapter 8
Collective Responsibility

There is a deep deception that exists on this planet and it is the idea that we are all evil at our deepest level. We often hear the statement that we all have a little Hitler inside us just waiting for the right moment to come out. This is a lie that has been fed to us by the people who do have a Hitler inside them. By normalizing their behaviour and making it look like everyone is capable of the same behaviour, they have managed to hide their presence among us. I am talking about the narcissists and psychopaths among us, who in reality are fallen beings that do not belong on this planet. These are the people who introduced the evil we see all around us on the planet. The only way these beings will leave this planet is when we decide that we do not want their consciousness on this planet. This reality has been hidden from humanity for a very long time and it is the true reason why we have evil on this planet. This may sound like a conspiracy theory to people who are unwilling to accept that there is more than meets the eye on this planet. Anyone who takes the time to analyse the behaviour of the globalists cannot miss the fact that their behaviour is truly abnormal. They are more like predators preying on humanity than fellow human beings simply making the wrong choices. The reality is that these beings are not like the rest of us and they work very hard to hide their presence from us. The thing they fear more than anything is exposure because they know that if their presence is discovered, humanity will experience a mass awakening and they will have to leave this planet. Once we understand this, then we realize that we truly have all the power and they have none. Their only power comes from deception, lies and keeping the planet in a perpetual state of fear. As long as we are afraid, we will never challenge their authority and as long as we don't challenge their authority, they will continue ruling over us. Having this knowledge should help us finally understand why the planet is in the state it is in and why we are in a perpetual state of war even though there is never any justification for war. By normalising violence, they make it appear as if we are all innately violent. But we know that non-narcissistic and non-psychopathic people are not violent by nature and have to be conditioned to accept violence.

When is war going to end on this planet? It will end only when a majority of us decide that we have had enough of war and do something about it. As long as the majority is silent, the minority will continue having their way every single time. They will continue manipulating us with nonsensical arguments and justifications for war and they will continue killing our sons and daughters in pursuit of their delusional agendas. This will only stop when we have had enough. Nothing positive has ever happened on this planet without the majority standing up to the minority and driving the change. Unless we stand up and demand our rights, the global elites will continue to trample us underfoot and take away our freedoms. This is the unfortunate fact of life on this planet and the sooner we accept it the better. As long as we don't rise up against them, they will continue to enslave us. These people are constantly working day and night to find ways to deceive humanity. We have to understand this and realize that we will not be free by remaining passive. The people trying to enslave us are not passive about their agenda. Being truly awake demands that we open our eyes to see the kind of planet we live on, one that is inhabited by fallen beings that are intent on our enslavement.

Our collective responsibility, therefore, is to awaken to the presence of fallen beings on our planet and to decide that we have had enough of their fallen consciousness. We must make the conscious decision to reject the consciousness of war and the idea that we are separate from our brothers and sisters in other parts of the world. We must not allow the fallen beings to continue dividing and conquering us by turning us against each other. The only way we prevail is by seeing ourselves as one people, one planet and one race - humanity. Fighting each other based on race, religion and ideologies is a distraction that keeps us from seeing what is happening, which is that we are all being manipulated by people who are not part of us. Failure to see this means we will continue fighting each other while the fallen beings continue winning.

International solidarity

One of the ways we can unite to push back against the relentless attacks on humanity is through international solidarity. The reason we still have wars on this planet is that many of us have chosen to ignore our governments' actions in other countries. Our attitude is that so long as our own lives are not impacted, we do not need to concern ourselves with what our governments are doing. Unfortunately, this attitude not only allows governments to trample over the rights of other people but in the long run, it boomerangs right back to us as the law of karma comes into effect. We cannot hurt other people and not expect that this will come back to us eventually. When your government attacks another country, don't assume that this has nothing to do with you. It has everything to do with you because sooner or later, your country will start reaping what it has sown and this will affect you personally. The pain that other people feel when they are bombed and their children murdered will eventually come back to haunt you. Therefore, resisting your government's attacks on other people is enlightened self-interest. It means that you understand that we are all connected and that the law of karma is inescapable. Remember, just because karma is delayed does not mean it will never come.

A good example of the law of karma at work is the backfiring of the sanctions the West imposed on Russia. Westerners in Europe are experiencing what it feels like to lack basic necessities due to their leaders' actions. They are experiencing directly what it feels like to have a brutal government that does not care whether they live or starve and freeze to death. This should enable Westerners understand what their governments have been doing to the rest of the world while they stood by and did nothing. When British people look back with nostalgia at the days of empire when most of the world was under British rule, I hope they will now understand what it feels like to be under a brutal tyrant. When Westerners sit back and do nothing while their governments bomb other countries in the name of freedom and democracy, I hope they will begin to understand what it feels like to be under siege. When Westerners sit back and do nothing while their governments apply sanctions on people in other countries, I hope they will begin to understand the sheer cruelty of these sanctions. They should ask themselves what the victims of their governments' wars and sanctions have been experiencing. How do the people of Iraq, Afghanistan, Syria, Yemen and Somalia feel when Western bombs rain down on them? Maybe Putin is the teacher the Westerners need to help them transcend their aggressive tendencies.

International solidarity means that we do not ignore what our governments are doing to people in other countries. It means that you step outside your comfort zone and vigorously protest when your government tries to justify attacking another country. It means that you see through the lies that governments use to justify these attacks because you understand that nothing could justify the torture of human beings. It means that you act in enlightened self-interest because you understand that sooner or later, the law of karma is going to come into effect. If you're Russian, you should protest when your government attacks Ukraine. Do not sit back and continue living your life as if nothing unusual were happening. Do not wait until the violence lands at your doorstep to protest because by then it will be too late. We have been hearing reports of Russian men fleeing their country because they are being forced to join the military. These Russian men did not protest when their government invaded Ukraine, they did not protest when Ukrainian citizens were fleeing their country and they did not protest when their government was issuing nuclear threats to the rest of the world. They allowed their tyrannical leader to do whatever he wanted to Ukraine and they were too afraid to stand up to him. They acted as if what was happening to Ukraine had nothing to do with them. Now, it is finally dawning on them that their government's actions have everything to do with them. They should have protested earlier, not waited until they were being forcefully conscripted to finally react. In the same way, Europeans watched as their governments imposed sanctions on Russia, acting as if it had nothing to do with them. They are finally protesting as the sanctions backfire on them, but it is too late. They have allowed their governments to exercise tyranny in other lands, never dreaming that this tyranny would eventually come back to them. They are experiencing the shock of being the victims of their tyrannical leaders and the ruthlessness of these leaders who will not negotiate with Russia to restore gas supplies. The lesson here is that we should never ignore the actions of our governments against other people because sooner or later, these same actions will be applied to us. When the law of karma goes into effect, we will not be spared but will experience the same pain that our governments have imposed on other people.

Regional solidarity

Regional solidarity can happen when countries that share common interests come together to form organisations that promote their mutual interests. With regard to war, these organisations play an important role in promoting peace and speaking out against war. For example, in Africa, we have the African Union (AU) which regularly speaks out against the wars breaking out on the continent. Apart from speaking out, the AU also sends representatives and delegates who help bring the warring parties to the table to negotiate. I mentioned in a previous chapter how the AU sent a representative to Kenya to help mediate the peaceful settlement of the post-election violence of 2007. We have seen the AU speak out against the various coups happening in West Africa and the civil war in Ethiopia. The AU has been instrumental in designating eminent African leaders as peace ambassadors who are helping calm a continent that has been embroiled in civil wars and instability for a very long time. I consider the AU a prime example of regional solidarity that can be emulated by other regions. There has unfortunately been a marked lack of condemnation of dangerous wars like the Russia-Ukraine war by regional blocs in the West. There is simply no one calling for peace apart from a few anti-war organisations. The only voices we hear are the aggressive voices of NATO, the European Union and the United

States. It seems that there is no regional body that is independent enough to call for peace. This allows wars to continue unabated while the narratives of the Western governments go unchallenged. In this regard, the BRICS (Brazil, Russia, India, China and South Africa) regional grouping has failed in its responsibility to speak out when one of their own invaded a neighbouring country. It doesn't matter what justification Russia gave for invading Ukraine; at the end of the day, war can never be justified by any argument. The BRICS should have tried to broker peace between the two countries, but instead, they stood by and watched as one of their members slid into a destructive war. How do they expect to continue having economic cooperation while one of their own is embroiled in a war? The silence of the BRICS and their inability to bring the two countries to the negotiating table is one of the most unfortunate aspects of the Russia-Ukraine war.

Apart from the AU, another regional body in Africa that plays an important role in promoting peace is the ECOWAS (Economic Community of West African States) which regularly speaks out against the coups and civil wars taking place in West Africa. Such bodies should be encouraged in their peace-supporting efforts because there can be no economic development without peace. In East Africa, we have the East African Community (EAC) while in Southern Africa we have the Southern Africa Development Community (SADC). These regional bodies could do more to promote peace and speak out against wars on the continent.

The dark side of regional cooperation is seen when institutions come together for the sole purpose of promoting war and aggression. A good example is NATO (North Atlantic Treaty Organisation) which serves no other purpose than to keep the world on a permanent war footing and AUKUS (Australia, United Kingdom, United States), which is geared towards opposing China. These bodies in effect create the very conditions they were created to prevent. Without war, these bodies would lose their purpose which means that they must constantly stoke tensions to remain relevant. Such bodies should be dissolved with immediate effect. The EU (European Union) started with noble intentions but has also failed in its duty to promote peace in Europe. During the tense Russia-Ukraine war, the EU has been the most aggressive proponent of punitive sanctions against Russia. Even when the sanctions failed and started causing suffering to European citizens, the EU did not change its stance. This is an unfortunate misuse of its regional position and is an example of the path that should be avoided by such bodies. Instead of promoting peace and prosperity for Europeans, the EU is today causing instability and lowered living standards. This is unacceptable.

Global solidarity

Global solidarity will only happen on this planet when we begin to see ourselves as part of the same human family. As long as we allow our differences to pull us apart, we will never see the peace and prosperity we all long for. We have allowed ourselves to be manipulated by forces that emphasize our differences in order to divide and conquer us. We need to understand that as long as some among us remain destitute, then the planet will always default to the lowest common denominator. It is as simple as that. The West has been deceived into believing that they can shut themselves in their developed enclaves and ignore the misery of the rest of the planet and all will be well. They have been deceived into thinking that the poor parts of the planet have nothing to do with them. They have been deceived into despising their brothers and sisters in less developed countries and blaming them for their misery. What Westerners need to understand is that this is the oldest trick in the book, the divide and conquer tactic. So long as you divide people and turn them against each other, you can control them. What the elites have done is allow the West to enjoy an illusory abundance in order to get them to support the system that gives them this abundance while keeping other countries down. Meanwhile, the elites get to keep for themselves the lion's share of everything. Because Westerners think of themselves as wealthy, they have supported a system that enslaves them and takes away more and more of their freedoms. By the time Westerners wake up to the deception, it will be too late. They will realize too late that we have all been robbed, all been deceived and all been denied by the same global elites. We are all victims of the same elites. If they have allowed Westerners to enjoy an illusory prosperity that is not true prosperity, it is because it suits their need to maintain the status quo. As Europeans are discovering today with the collapse of their energy supply and food supply, the elites do not care about them or anybody else. They will destroy Westerners as easily as they destroy other people on the planet. If Westerners had stood in solidarity with the global south as they were being destroyed, they would not be experiencing the same destruction today. Instead, they stood by and watched as their governments attacked and invaded other countries, they stood by and watched as their governments enslaved and colonized other countries and they stood by and watched as their leaders insulted other countries. They thought they were superior, not realizing that they were as much slaves of their psychopathic leaders as anyone else. Today, these same leaders have turned on them and started the process of destroying them.

The lesson we need to learn as citizens of the planet is that we should never stand by and watch as our brothers and sisters in any part of the world are being mistreated. We should not allow a situation whereby our leaders spend billions of dollars on the military while people in other parts of the world lack basics like food, shelter and medical care. We have to learn to reject the divisions that have been imposed upon us by the elites. The reason they work so hard to divide us is that they cannot win against a united front. The only reason they keep winning is that we are too busy fighting each other to see what ails us. Whenever war breaks out in any part of the world, we must speak out against it. We must stand with our brothers and sisters in all parts of the planet and see them as one with us. The undeniable reality is that we are all connected and whatever happens in any part of the world affects all other parts of the world. Anything that is done to anyone anywhere affects everyone on the planet. The sooner we begin to see this, the better. The sooner we discard the idea that we can do evil to people in faraway places and that it has no impact on us, the higher we can rise as a planet. This is the true genius of our creator. By connecting all of us to each other, he put in place the conditions that would help us learn to care for each other. The only way we will prosper as a planet is when we start caring for everyone the way we care for ourselves.

The United Nations

The United Nations was established on 24 October 1945 after the second world war, in an attempt to bring the world together in peaceful coexistence. According to its Charter, the UN aims:

"to save succeeding generations from the scourge of war, …to reaffirm faith in fundamental human rights, …to establish conditions under which justice and respect for the obligations arising from treaties and other sources of international law can be maintained, and to promote social progress and better standards of life in larger freedom"

Despite its good intentions, the UN has struggled to meet its lofty mandate and one of the reasons is that it was dominated from the very beginning by countries that were more concerned with control and dominance than with truly serving the planet. The struggle for dominance culminated in the creation of the veto vote, which is one of the structural issues that has prevented the UN from fulfilling its mandate. The United States, United Kingdom, Russia, France and China make up the five permanent members of the Security Council and each of them has a veto vote. The veto vote makes it virtually impossible for the UN to pass any resolutions or take any action that is unpopular with any of the five permanent members of the Security Council. While the United Nations has great potential in helping resolve the many problems facing the planet, this potential has not been realized mainly because the five members hold the organisation back and prevent action on anything they deem contrary to their interests. Instead of focusing on the interests of the planet as a whole, they have turned the United Nations into a forum for flexing their muscles and showing off their power. Until the UN resolves the issue of the veto vote and ends the dominance of the Security Council, it will struggle to meet its mandate. The beautiful words in its charter will remain just that, beautiful words that have no bearing on reality. This capture of the United Nations, not just by the Security Council but by other interests has turned it into a bureaucratic monstrosity that functions slowly and makes no difference in global events. For example, the World Health Organisation, one of the arms of the United Nations has been captured by Bill Gates and is being used to push the globalists' agenda. This capture has made the United Nations a body where beautiful, moving speeches are given but nothing ever comes out of them. For the UN to meet its mandate, the countries that make up the majority would need to insist on a change in its structure and deal with the globalist capture of the organisation.

The General Assembly is the part of the UN that embodies the true spirit of cooperation that the UN has the potential to manifest. The General Assembly has been instrumental in addressing many of the problems that the Security Council was not interested in including decolonization, the independence of Namibia, apartheid in South Africa, terrorism, the AIDS epidemic and denuclearisation. The General Assembly has raised awareness of the many problems facing the planet and has passed many resolutions to deal with them. This is the true spirit of the United Nations. Unfortunately, the Security Council continues to hold the UN back with its focus on militarization, its sabotage when it comes to issues touching on any of its members and outright refusal to cooperate on issues that the Security Council members do not want to deal with. An example of this is the Treaty on the Prohibition of Nuclear Weapons. While the majority of countries in the UN have already signed on to this treaty, none of the permanent Security Council members who are all nuclear-armed countries has signed the treaty. This means that the UN cannot do anything on this very important topic of banning nuclear weapons on the planet. Another example is in the current Russia-Ukraine war whereby Russia has repeatedly vetoed any attempt to pass any resolution criticizing its actions. On this particular issue, the impartiality of the United Nations is also called into question because while it is willing to criticize Russia for invading Ukraine, it has remained silent on the actions of the United States and NATO in escalating the war by sending massive amounts of weapons into Ukraine. If the United Nations hopes to have an impact on the planet, it has to remain impartial and equally censure anyone who violates its peace-keeping efforts.

As a global peace-keeping body, the UN should be at the forefront of diplomatic efforts whenever any of its members are involved in conflicts. The UN should be a promoter of dialogue, de-escalation and détente. Instead, what we observe is that the UN remains silent while wars break out or spends weeks trying to come up with the right wording to condemn the parties to the conflict without offending any of the powerful nations. This is a complete sham and a dereliction of its duty. The UN must come out strongly in support of peace in any conflict in any part of the world. They must send peace delegations to try to bring warring parties to the table. When the Russia-Ukraine war started, only Turkey attempted to bring the warring parties to the table for negotiations. Meanwhile, the UN was engaged in an attempt to craft a resolution that did not offend the West. The UN has been completely useless in the Russia-Ukraine war, just as it has been useless in stopping or preventing any war on the planet. This is truly a disgrace for a body that has so much potential to bring peace to the planet. Rather than promoting diplomacy, negotiation and de-escalation, what the UN does is stand by and do nothing while wars are starting, then later send "peace-keeping troops." I already discussed in earlier chapters the lie of the peace-keeping troops. It is like pouring fuel in the fire instead of water and acting as if both can achieve the same thing. It is not logical. Soldiers are trained to fight not to bring peace. This is a clear indication that the UN has been captured by globalists. The UN cannot be described as a peace-keeping institution because its behaviour is not that of an institution that is interested in peace. All it does is give the appearance of working for peace with its many conferences while in reality doing nothing to promote peace. Any honest analysis of the UN will come to this conclusion. The only redeeming quality of the UN is the General Assembly, but this is nothing but a toothless bulldog. The solution at this point appears to be the formation of a new global body that truly supports and promotes peace. The countries in the UN that make up the majority must come together and create a new body that can do what the UN only pretends to do. The UN must be abandoned en masse and a new body created that serves the interests of the planet rather than the interests of the globalists. This can be the beginning of true global solidarity that will move the planet forward.

Chapter 9
A World Without War

Is a world without war possible? We have been led to believe that this is not possible. We are asked to believe without question that countries have always been at war and will always be at war. We are asked to accept that human beings are inherently violent and will always engage in violent confrontations against each other. But this is demonstrably untrue. Most people exist in harmony with each other in their neighbourhoods, workplaces and communities. While we all disagree with others at some point, these disagreements rarely turn violent. Most people live their entire lives never having shown any desire for or tendency towards violence. Violent people such as the ones who abuse their spouses or who start fights in bars are the exception rather than the rule. Most people are decidedly not violent in their day-to-day lives, and yet we are asked to believe and accept that we are all inherently violent. The truth is that there is a violent subset among us, a tiny minority that unfortunately has managed to drag the rest of us down with them. Human beings have to be coerced, lied to and brainwashed to get them to go to war with each other. Violence is not part of our natural makeup and we need to reject the idea that we are inherently violent. When we see through the deception that brought us where we are and understand that we are constantly being manipulated, we will be able to end the cycle of violence on our planet. A world without war is possible.

The most patent proof that a world without war is possible can be seen from the observable fact that no one bothers the most peaceful countries. Countries that do not have a military force seem to do just fine. This exposes the lie that every country must have a standing army to guard against some external threat. The truth is that there is no external threat and there never has been. Those that want war have to work hard to bring about the conditions necessary for war, including lying to their citizens and carrying out false flag events. The United States and NATO have been working hard for a long time to provoke war with Russia and their efforts are finally paying off. September 11 was a false flag event which was used to justify the war on terror. The fact is that war is never justified and it never happens spontaneously. War is not an inevitable fact of life but is caused by aggressive people looking for trouble. Therefore, we can conclude that war is a choice. And if it is a choice, then all we have to do is choose differently to have peace on the planet. We can begin to choose peace today and reject the consciousness of war and violence on this planet.

Fighting imaginary enemies

When we start understanding how the world works and start seeing through the narratives perpetuated by the mainstream media, it becomes immediately obvious that a lot of work goes into starting wars. It takes years, even decades to get people to hate another country enough to go to war with them. In their natural state, people do not just start hating another country. They have to be thoroughly propagandized and brainwashed into believing that a country presents a threat to them. We have seen this happening over the years in the West where Russia and China have been demonized and turned into an existential threat that has to be dealt with. If you were observant, you may have noticed the anxiety in the West when it became clear that China was going to overtake America as the foremost economic power. This anxiety quickly turned into hostility with economic wars being waged against China and eventually, NATO declared China an emerging threat to the West. Within about a decade, China went from being a competitor to an existential threat that needed to be contained. In reality, China does not present any existential threat to the West. The only unpardonable sin that China committed was to threaten the West's hegemony. That is the real reason why the West is looking for an excuse to go to war with China. The provocations surrounding Taiwan are an excuse for the West to destroy China. In the same way, Russia does not pose any existential threat to the West. The only sin they committed is in protecting their economy from the globalists who wanted unfettered access to their national resources. The greed of the globalists is insatiable and anyone who stands in their way instantly becomes an enemy to be destroyed. Every war that has ever been fought by the West is done for profit and to subdue countries that refuse to submit.

What then do we learn from this? We learn that the world is busy fighting imaginary enemies that are created by the very people who benefit from war. There is no truth to the idea that the world is full of enemies trying to attack a country. There is no truth to the idea that every country needs to have a standing army ready to fight external enemies. This is a false narrative that is created to serve the globalists and their endless greed for profit. The world is constantly wasting resources fighting imaginary enemies when those resources could be used for the good of the people. The sad reality of our planet is that we exist in a make-believe world created by delusional psychopaths. Institutions such as NATO, AUKUS and the CIA work tirelessly to maintain this make-believe world. Politicians are hopelessly caught up in the web of lies because of the financial benefits they reap from this sad state of affairs. With the mainstream media completely under the control of the elites, the masses have no hope of seeing through the complex deception. The only hope is that the few who have woken up to the deception will awaken their brothers and sisters who are still asleep. Once a critical mass of people sees through the deception, we will be able to dismantle the almost unimaginable web of deception that the globalists have woven. Since this construct is unreal and requires massive amounts of lies and deception to maintain, it means that it cannot last forever and will eventually collapse. We are yet to see tyranny that lasts forever. Every tyrannical structure eventually breaks down because a structure that is based on deception is like a house that is built on sinking sand. It is only a matter of time before it collapses.

Mutually Assured Destruction

Mutually Assured Destruction or MAD is a doctrine of nuclear deterrence that posits that if two opponents each have sufficient destructive capabilities to annihilate each other, then none of them will attack the other for fear of being annihilated. The MAD doctrine assumes that all actors in a conflict are rational and therefore will be motivated by the avoidance of annihilation. Our analysis of the people who are behind wars unfortunately shows that they are not rational actors. These people are psychopaths who lie constantly and go to great lengths to deceive the masses into going to war for the sake of profits.   These people do not value human life and have no compunction about killing millions of people to serve their agendas. The idea that these people can be trusted to avoid nuclear war is delusional. If pushed to a corner, they will not hesitate to use nuclear weapons. It would be naïve to assume that countries maintaining massive amounts of nuclear weapons will never use them. Have you ever wondered why the elites spend so much on underground bunkers? It is because they know for a fact that nuclear weapons will be used one day. The only people who believe that nuclear weapons can never be used are the masses who are lulled into a false sense of security by the mainstream media. Nuclear weapons are a constant danger to humanity that must be eliminated before the psychopaths decide to use them. It is only a matter of time before this happens.

To demonstrate just how unrealistic the MAD doctrine is, consider the US doctrine of full spectrum dominance or the Wolfowitz doctrine. These two doctrines directly contradict each other. The Wolfowitz doctrine sees the US as the only superpower whose main objective is to retain that position and to prevent the emergence of any other superpower at any cost. In order to maintain its superpower position, the US will do everything in its power to destroy any country that challenges this position. Naturally, we can assume that this includes the use of nuclear weapons, otherwise why spend so much of its resources on nuclear weapons? Once we understand that globalists are psychopaths, then we can begin to understand that they do not fear the annihilation of human life. When pushed to a corner where their dominance is under threat, they would rather blow up the whole planet than accept defeat. Their desire for dominance will override the MAD doctrine any day. Anyone who is keenly observing the events unfolding today should know by now that nuclear war is inevitable. The psychopaths in the West and their puppet Zelensky are not interested in negotiating. President Putin will not be bullied into giving in to the West. It should be clear to everyone that the MAD doctrine will not deter these people. We must understand that as long as nuclear weapons exist on this planet, their use is a question of when not if. The path towards a world without war must begin with the dismantling of nuclear arsenals.

What goes around comes around

I have talked about the law of karma in previous chapters, but this is something that cannot be over-emphasised. Although human beings have a vague idea about karma, they do not seem to understand that this is a spiritual law that is just as real as the law of gravity. We all understand and accept the law of gravity as an unavoidable law of nature. Everything that goes up must come down. This law works whether we believe in it or not – it does not seek our permission before coming into effect. If you jump out the window of a tall building without a parachute, you will surely land on the ground, with the attendant consequences. We understand that the creator's laws work whether we want them to or not, yet for some strange reason, we have chosen to ignore the law of karma and try to live as if it does not exist. Some of us do not believe in karma - we just assume that things happen the way they do because of forces beyond our control. But like every other law that has been put in place by our creator, the law of karma does not care whether we believe in it or not. It is constantly working in our lives whether we like it or not and we cannot run away from it or wish it away. Our best bet is to learn how it works and live in ways that do not bring us into conflict with this law.

One of the major misunderstandings about the law of karma is that it is meant to punish us. This is not the case. The law of karma is meant to be our teacher. This law allows us to have experiences that bring about our learning. For example, if you keep hurting people, it means that you need to learn that human beings are interconnected, meaning that you cannot hurt others without hurting yourself. The law of karma brings about situations in your life which help you learn this lesson. It is not a punishment but an opportunity to learn. We could say that the law of karma acts as a mirror that shows you the hidden things you are not able to see about yourself. Another misunderstanding about the law of karma is that karma should happen instantly. In other words, if you do something wrong, then karma should hit you instantly like lightning. When we do not observe an instant consequence to our actions, we assume that the law of karma is not real. But this is not the way karma works. The way karma works is that you are given a grace period during which you can learn your lessons the easy way. In other words, you are allowed to transcend your state of consciousness without necessarily having to experience the consequences of your actions in the physical world. This is why many people dismiss the law of karma as unreal because it appears as if people can do whatever they want and get away with it. What we need to understand is that we are all given an opportunity to learn our lessons the easy way, for example through the teachings of Christ or the Buddha or the many other teachings that exist on the planet. It is only when we show that we are not willing to learn from our teachers that we must learn the hard way. These lessons might manifest even several lifetimes down the line. No one gets away with unbalanced actions even though it might appear as if they are doing so. If they refuse to learn the easy way, they will eventually have to learn through the hard knocks.

Many of us are unwilling to learn in any other way except through hard knocks. This is unfortunate because it is much easier to learn from the spiritual teachings available on the planet than through karma manifesting in our lives. But if we show ourselves unwilling to learn in any other way, then we must experience our karma. This law applies at the personal level and the collective level as well. The most aggressive countries will eventually attract an opposite and equal force that will act as the teacher they need to teach them the lessons they refuse to learn. Countries in the West, notably the United States, the United Kingdom and France have long acted in cruel, unbalanced ways, spreading terror and violence everywhere they go. For a long time, it seemed as if they were getting away with it, but in reality, they were just being given time to transcend their consciousness without having to experience the consequences of their actions. Sooner or later, however, the chickens will come home to roost. I have mentioned in previous chapters some of the ways this is happening. By being on the receiving end for once, hopefully, they will understand what other countries experience when they impose their cruel sanctions on them.

Laying down our weapons

Human beings have been fighting each other for a very long time. Surely, it must be clear by now that violence doesn't work. War does not accomplish anything other than laying the foundation for the next war. War is a meaningless activity whose only purpose is the mindless destruction of our precious planet. All war does is pull us downwards and waste the energy that could be used to build our planet. And the worst part is, we do it all for the benefit of a few psychopaths and their lunatic ideologies. We the people are the ones who truly pay the price for war - the ordinary people who are displaced from their homes, who lose their loved ones and whose lives are stolen from them at their prime when they should be at their most creative. All this so that a few people can make more money and gain more power. When will we start seeing through the lie that is war? When are we going to say enough of the bloodshed, we do not want to fight anymore. We will only know peace on this planet when we decide that we have had enough, we are not willing to be used anymore and we will not take up arms against our brothers and sisters. It starts with YOU. The world will only change when each of us individually decides to change our worldview, change our beliefs and change our actions. Do not look at other people thinking that the world will change when *they* change their worldview. Start by changing yourself. Examine your worldview, your beliefs and your actions. If there is even an iota of violence in you, work on yourself. If you are holding on to any beliefs that justify war for any reason whatsoever, let go of those beliefs. Remember Jesus' words:

But I say to you, do not resist an evil person; but whoever slaps you on your right cheek, turn the other to him also.

Matthew 5:39

Until you accept Jesus' words as the only truth that will pull this planet out of war, we will never know peace. Peace comes when we internalize the concept of turning the other cheek. Peace will come when we internalize the spirit of Nelson Mandela or Mahatma Gandhi that no matter what you do to me, I will not respond with violence. When you accept this truth, then you will have done your part in pulling up the collective consciousness. As we are all interconnected, when you raise your consciousness, you will pull up the collective consciousness and make it easier for others to see through the lies. Therefore, work on yourself, resolve your own false beliefs and raise your consciousness. This is truly the best service you can give to the planet. It is time we laid down our weapons and walked away from the battlefield.

Follow my blog for updates on new publications:

https://violetflame.home.blog